FREE
Stuff &
Good Deals
for Your
Pet

by Linda Bowman

SANTA
MONICA
PRESS

Published by:
SANTA MONICA PRESS LLC
P.O. Box 1076
Santa Monica, CA 90406-1076
1-800-784-9553
www.santamonicapress.com

Printed in the United States

Santa Monica Press books are available at special quantity discounts when purchased in bulk by corporations, organizations, or groups. Please call our Special Sales department at 1-800-784-9553.

This book is intended to provide general information. The publisher, author, distributor, and copyright owner are not engaged in rendering health, medical, legal, financial, or other professional advice or services. Be aware that offers, phone numbers, addresses, web sites, etc. may have changed. The publisher, author, distributor, and copyright owner are not liable or responsible to any person or group with respect to any loss, illness, or injury caused or alleged to be caused by the information found in this book.

ISBN 1-891661-14-0

Library of Congress Cataloging-in-Publication Data

Bowman, Linda, 1947-
        Free stuff & good deals for your pet / by Linda Bowman
        p. cm.
        ISBN 1-891661-14-0 (pbk.)
        1. Pets—Computer network resources—Directories. 2. Internet addresses—Directories. 3. Free material—Directories. I. Title: Free stuff and good deals for your pet. II. Title.
        SF411.5 .B68 2001
        025.06'6360887—dc21

                                                        00-069692

Book and cover design by Lynda "Cool Dog" Jakovich
Illustrations by Jorge Pacheco

Contents

INTRODUCTION

The Family Pet

People simply love their family pets. We play with them, ride them, cuddle with them, travel with them, exercise with them, depend on them, sing to them, talk to them and scold them. They are truly cherished members of our family.

Not unlike children, their care and feeding can become an expensive investment over the long run. Veterinary bills, food and vitamin bills, bills for toys and treats, supplies (bedding, blankets, shampoos, conditioners, collars, bridles, shoes saddles, cages and so on) all add up. The list of what we spend on our pets seems never-ending. A survey has shown that in the next decade pet related spending will increase by as much as 30 percent, totaling more than $15 billion. Expenditures on pet food has increased from $5.5 billion in the early 1990s to over $7 billion today. Some pet food industry experts estimate the amount spent is even higher, nearing the $8 billion mark.

More than ever, the pet marketplace is flooded with an endless stream of products. For example, there are more than 90 brands of cat food available in the U.S. today. Whether we own fancy gold fish or Kentucky Fox Trotters, most of us would like to give our pets "the best that money can buy," but not all of us can afford to. In the blink of an eye, we pet owners easily spend hundreds and often thousands of dollars a year taking care of our furry, feathered, four-legged and waterbound friends.

As a pet owner (three dogs, one cat, thirteen koi and two horses) I have always looked for savings in pet shops, feed stores and magazine advertisements. What I discovered is that there is a tremendous array of little known free and low cost products and services available for our domestic friends. The trick is to know where and how to find these great discounts and savings. Even if raising children in today's world costs 'an arm and a leg,' raising and caring for our animals doesn't have to.

This book will provide you with the information you need to take advantage of incredible free services and products for pets. I also have included information that will guarantee you substantial savings when a freebie just isn't possible. Whether you have cats, dogs, fish, birds or horses, you can begin enjoying your animals even more with the bargains contained in this book. In addition, I have included sources for savings on things for pet lovers and pet owners, too. Jewelry, clothing, doormats, stickers, stamps, calendars, mugs and hats emblazoned with your favorite breed are just some of the thousands of goodies and gifts available to animal lovers.

We will start with the basic issue of where and how you can get a pet, often a purebred or pedigree, for absolutely free. You may not be aware of the many sources of locating fine, loving animals in need of good homes. Once you have brought your new pet home, you will want to give him/her the best possible care to insure health, happiness and a long life.

You don't have to go back to school or take courses to learn how to care for your animals. Everything you've ever wanted to know about the care, feeding and health of your pet(s) can be learned from the sources that we refer you to in this book. There are hundreds of free pamphlets, books, articles and publications produced by manufacturers of pet products, animal protection associations, organizations and practitioners in the fields of animal health services. In fact, there is so much free information out there that, in many cases, you can solve your pet's problems and save on expensive veterinary bills by referring to these excellent, informative sources before spending your money unnecessarily.

Of course, some professionally administered medical treatments must be given to insure your pet's ongoing health and immunity against common diseases. These preventive measures are not only important for your pets (and required by law), but they also protect owners from contracting diseases transmittable between humans and animals. These vaccines and treatments can add up to a lot of money; however, there are ways of saving on these costs and sometimes even getting these services for free-if you know how.

Some pets are finiky eaters. Others will gobble anything you put in front of them and ask for more. Different kinds of animals require different kinds of diets and nutritional considerations. A professional show dog or cat may require a different diet than a family pet. A competing hunter-jumper or cross-country competition horse may need supplements and vitamins not necessary for an average trail or pleasure horse. Today, most animal professionals agree that pet food should be selected depending upon the pet's age and health (puppy/kitten, adult/maintenance, older/less active/mature, over-weight/underweight). How can you find out what kind of diet is best for your animal? Most pet food manufacturers are more than happy to provide you with free samples of their products. In fact, there is no reason you should spend your money just to try their products. Pet stores, veterinary offices and pet shows abound with free samples of the largest, most nutritionally advanced formulas.

Another way to save money is by clipping cou-pons from your daily Saturday or Sunday newspaper coupon section. Because of the fierce competition between major supermarket brand pet foods, high value (and free) coupon offers have become a common method for luring new customers. Since most supermarkets double manufacturers coupons, those $.50 to $1.50 coupons can add up to great savings at the checkout counter, whether you're testing new brands or buying your regular pet food. Even "gourmet" pet food producers have gotten into the coupon act by advertising discounts and savings in pet magazines and newsletters.

You will also find great savings for many other pet services. Pet grooming, flea control, pet-sitting, training, boarding facilities and pet insurance are important services many of us need at one time or another. The more you know about these services, the more you can save when you choose which ones are best suited for you and your pet.

Are you interested in learning or doing more for the pet and animal community in your area? There are dozens of worthwhile organizations whose purposes are to protect and support the animal population of this country. We will introduce you to some of these important and interesting organizations whose continuing efforts are enhancing the quality of life for our pets and animals.

The more you know and learn about your pets, the better a "pet parent" you will be for them. To help you achieve this goal, we have included a variety of animal magazines, newsletters, books and book publishers. In most cases, we will show you how to get free sample issues and discounts on these valuable publications.

One of the best ways to compare and save on products for our pets is by shopping from mail-order catalogs. There are literally hundreds of catalogs with thousands of items for pets and pet lovers. Most of these catalogs are available free and many offer items at substantial savings. Why not do your comparison shopping from the comfort of your home? Your research will pay off handsomely in the dollars you'll save by finding the lowest prices and best values.

Better yet, do your comparison shopping over the Internet. Sites for pet products abound. This is one of the most competitive retail areas on the World Wide Web. Special offers, discounts, free shipping and more are some of the ways online pet sites are trying to entice shoppers to try buying from them. And once they have you as a customer, they want you to keep coming back. Online catalogs and brick and mortar chain stores that have established web sites all want your business and are willing to give you more for your money to get it.

Free stuff for your pet is all around you. Great savings on quality products and services are there for the asking. By becoming a smart shopper and using the information in the following chapters, you can enjoy many years with happy, healthy pets in your home and extra cash in your pocket!

CHAPTER 1

How to Get a Pet for Free

The greatness of a nation and its moral progress can be judged by the way its animals are treated.
—Mohandas Karamchand Gandhi

Public Shelters and Pounds

Adopting a pet through city or county departments of Animal Regulation or Animal Care and Control shelters is an easy, economical way to bring a pet into your home. Unwanted, lost, stray and abandoned animals of every shape, size, age and breed can be found at your local shelter waiting for a good home. More than 15 million pets end up in animal shelters each year and nearly 11 million of those are "put to sleep." About 30 percent of these animals are "pure-breds," the majority coming from what are commonly referred to as "backyard breeders" and the "Midwest puppy mills" found in Kansas, Iowa, Missouri, Arkansas, Nebraska, Oklahoma and Pennsylvania.

These public shelters can't possibly place all the animals that are found or brought to them. Even privately funded shelters, such as local Humane Societies or SPCAs (Society for the Prevention of Cruelty to Animals), have a difficult time finding homes and human companionship for their rescued, unwanted animals. For example, a typical Humane Society shelter in a major metropolitan area might house as many as 18,000 pets a year, but, on an average, can only find homes for 1,200 of them. In many of these shelters the animals are free. In others the shelters charge an adoption fee to cover vaccinations, licenses (dogs only), medical exams, neutering or spaying-which can run between $35 and $100. In many cases, shelters offer free, discounted or low-cost services, collars and leashes, and cat carriers to qualifying senior citizens or people with low incomes. To help you select a puppy or dog from one of these groups, you may want to pick up a copy of *The Chosen Puppy or Secondhand Dog* by Carol Lea Benjamin, generally available at your local humane or anti-cruelty society and at this web site: www.dogbooks.com/adopt.htm.

Non-Profit Adoption Agencies and Rescue Groups

There are many organizations that rescue animals from shelters and care for them. World Animal Net at worldanimal.net/ maintains a listing of over 10,000 animal protection societies. Some groups will provide animals for free to qualified homes, others require some reimbursement for associated costs such as spaying and neutering. Some of these groups specialize in rescuing specific breeds, such as Akitas, Dobermans, Terriers, Alaskan Malamutes, Basset Hounds, Welsh Corgis, Scotties, Great Pyrenees, German Shepherds, etc. Often these purebreds are older or abused animals. Many come from puppy mills and ended up sick or abandoned with problems making them unsuitable for pet stores to sell. There are also many wonderful, healthy, happy purebreds who have ended up in shelters for a variety of reasons and that make excellent companions. An extensive listing of dog rescue groups by breed can be found at www.faqs.org/faqs/dogs-faq/rescue and at www.critterhaven.org/critterchat/rescuenets.htm.

Rescue and Adoption Central www.petstation. com/central.htm has a very extensive, organized listing of open rescue and adoption groups that serve any or multiple pets; bird rescue groups; cat rescue groups; dog rescue groups classified by U.S. nationwide, regional, Canada and the U.K.; and listings for rescue groups for tortoises, horses, ferrets and rabbits.

Petsmart.com www.acmepet.petsmart.com/ has a database of rescues and shelters for all types of pets, including horses, birds, dogs, cats and exotic animals. Also available is a searchable database of veterinary clinics around the U.S. Through its Grants and Sponsorships Program, PETsMART Charities offers funding opportunities for qualified Animal Welfare Organizations. In 1999, PETsMART Charities raised and donated $4 million, making it the nation's leading supporter of pet groups. This site is currently gathering information on Dog Parks around the United States to add to its existing database. If there is a dog park in your area add it to the database. You can also search for dog parks around the U.S.

On a personal note, four years ago my husband brought home a 7-week old Collie puppy from the Collie Rescue Society. A female who was living in a home where she was abused had just given birth, and her rescuers took her and her pups away and raised them until they could be placed in good homes. Now, four years later, Barkley is the most wonderful, loving, intelligent dog we could ever imagine. He is also qualified and certified to be a Therapy Pet, which means he visits different care giving facilities, senior centers and camps making folks happy and spreading his love.

Senior dogs and cats make wonderful friends for children and older adults. Some animal rescue organizations (such as those found at the web sites www.srdogs.com and www.arescuemom.org) specialize in these kinds of pets, placing them in appropriate homes for free. Studies have shown that elderly people who own pets benefit both psychologically and physically from having a pet companion. The theory behind this is that pets provide comfort and companionship that older people might otherwise seek from physicians. For example, the Minnesota Valley Humane Society www.mvhspets.org began offering a 15 percent discount on pet adoption fees to seniors (age 60 and over) on the pet of their choice. It also participates in Purina's "Pets for People" program, where seniors may receive a free pet.

Parrot Rescue www.parrothouse.com/rescue.html is sponsored by a not-for-profit, international pet bird rescue/sanctuary organization for unwanted or abused birds with branches across the USA and Canada. The main objective of the site's authors is to offer free guidance to individuals wishing to purchase their first bird. They believe that if they can inform a potential new bird owner of the care, commitment, specie behavior and temperament of the bird before they purchase it, chances are the bird will not become unwanted in the future. The editors also offer free assistance to pet bird owners with problems they might be having with their birds.

Retired greyhounds make excellent, loving pets. Greyhounds that are no longer able to race or who are unsuitable for breeding purposes are destroyed unless rescued and adopted. There are a number of groups involved in rescuing greyhounds; many are national or international in scope with local chapters and some are simply regional groups. A number of them maintain web sites:

- www.adopt-a-greyhound.org/index.html provides links to web pages for greyhound adoption groups throughout the United States, Canada and also European groups.

- www.greyhound.org provides links to greyhound rescue, adoption and has an e-Zine. (Hopkinton, MA, 508-435-5969).

- Greyhound Rescue's web site is adopt-a-greyhound.org/ghr_md.html; e-mail ghr@adopt-a-greyhound.org.

- Recycled Racers has information about adopting a greyhound at 303-288-1591; write c/o Wembley Park, 6200 Dahlia, Commerce City, CO 80022, or e-mail at sandyajohn@aol.com.

- Greyhound Pets of America maintains a web site at www.gpa-nova.org/, 800-366-1472, PO Box 710141, Oak Hill, VA 20171, e-mail at GPAhound@aol.com. You may also e-mail for information at MrsGreyhound@dsdial.net

- USA Defenders of Greyhounds/Retired Racing Greyhounds has been operating since 1988. They take great care in placing greyhounds in appropriate homes. Contact them at: 317-290-5292 for a lengthy explanation of their program and an application to adopt.

At present there are over 50 greyhound race tracks in the U.S. Many tracks, such as the Phoenix Greyhound Park (www.phxgp.com/pets/adopt.html, 602-273-7181) offer retired racers for adoption for a fee, usually $150 which covers veterinary costs plus spaying and neutering.

The Flagler track in Florida, PO Box 350940, Miami, FL 33135, 954-925-7758, (www.flaglerdogs.com/adopt.html) offers greyhounds for adoption free right at the race track, but the owner is required to spay or neuter the dog. If you live near a track or are planning a vacation near one, ask whether it has an adoption program.

The web site nga.jc.net/tracks.htm has a comprehensive list of all the greyhound tracks with web sites. It provides addresses and phone numbers for tracks that do not maintain a web site.

There are several ways, aside from the Internet, to find out about local or regional rescue and adoption organizations. One is by checking with local veterinary clinics and pet stores (the ones that don't sell their own pets). They usually carry flyers or cards for these groups. You can find listings for city and county animal shelters in the government listing pages of your phone directory.

An extensive listing of animal welfare organizations can be found at www.cyberjockey.com/animals. htm.

World Animal Net, Boston, MA, 617-524-3670, maintains a web site at worldanimalnet.org, which contains an extensive listing of animal shelters and rescue groups, as does the American Veterinary Medical Association at www.avma.org/netvet/dogs. htm#rescue.

Pets4YouDirectory www.pets4you.com/ maintains a free directory of breeders and rescue organizations to help guide people in their search for a pet to fit their lifestyle.

Adoption Publications

Muttmatchers Messenger is a free paper, put out every two months, listing adoptable dogs throughout Southern California, with pictures. There are many purebreds as well as mixed breeds. Sources include both private parties and a variety of privately sponsored pet rescue groups. Examples of rescue shelters offering dogs for adoption includes Friends for Pets Foundation, Little Dog Adoption, Animal Alliance, Pet Orphans Fund, Lifeline for Pets, Humane Animal Rescue Team, Foundation for Indigent Animals, Neighborhood Adoption Group, Animal Alliance and Friends of Animals Foundation. Available at most pet-supply stores, or call 805-524-4542 or e-mail them at Muttmatch@aol.com.

Project BREED (Breed Rescue Efforts and Education Directory), www.pet-vet.com/pb.htm publishes a directory listing organizations that provide rescue services by breed 202-244-0065.

Cat Fancy magazine www.animalnetwork. com/cats/default.asp publishes periodic listings of shelters and rescue organizations. E-mail catfancy@ fancypubs.com.

wwwPetbond.com is a new adoption web site. If you're looking for a new pet or searching for a lost pet, check it out. They list pictures and information about animals from area shelters, rescue groups and private foster care. There's also an events section, answers to pet related questions, pet care columns by Vet Tech Alisa Merlin, and a message board.

Non-Profit Adoption Centers

In addition to rescuing pets from public animal shelters, many of the privately supported animal programs (and some humane societies) take in pets whose owners, for a variety of circumstances, are no longer able to care for them. These no-kill shelters fall into two groups: those that offer care for a pet until it is adopted, even if that care extends to the end of the animal's life; and those that offer lifetime care with a no-adoption option, a kind of "retirement home" for pets. Many of these are cageless, home-like environments where the animals live in a warm, secure, comfortable home until adoption. The cost of adopting these animals is usually minimal, just enough to defray medical and sterilization expenses. The following are examples of non-profit shelters that take in pets and care for them until they are adopted:

Pet Orphans Fund www.petorphansfund.org. Van Nuys, CA; 818-901-0190; 800-400-PETS.

Montana Large Animal Sanctuary and Rescue www.mtanimalsanctuary.com. PO Box 939, Polson, MT 59860-0939; 406-883-1823.

Hava Heart Sanctuary www.techline.com/~hava. PO Box 1913, Westport, WA 98595; 360-268-9092.

Noah's Ark Sanctuary www.noahsark2by2.org. 111 No First St., Rockford, IL 61107; 815-962-2767

Safe Haven Animal Sanctuary www.noahsark 2by2.org.

Best Friends Animal Sanctuary www.bestfriends. com. Kanab, UT; 435-644-2001.

Second Chance Animal Sanctuary secondchance. norman.ok.us Norman, OK; 405-321-1915.

Planned Pethood Homeward Bound www. plannedpethood.org. Whitehouse, OH; 419-877-FIXX.

National Humane Education Sanctuaries www.nhes.org/html/sanctuaries.htmlne. Leesburg, VA; 703-777-8319.

FISCO Animal shelters californiamall.com/ animal_shelters.htm.

Cat Care Society www.catcaresociety.org. Lakewood, CO; 303-239-9680.

North Shore Animal League www.nsal.org. Port Washington, NY; 516-883-7575.

American Society for the Prevention of Cruelty to Animals www.aspca.org. New York, NY; 212-876-7700.

Actors and Others for Animals www.actorsand others.com. 11523 Burbank Blvd., No. Hollywood, CA 91601; 818-755-6045.

A comprehensive directory by state of no-kill animal organizations can be found at www.save ourstrays.com/no-kill.htm.

An extensive listing by state of shelters is at www.nacard.com/morlistj.html.

Service and Guide Dogs

If you are interested in adopting a dog, you might want to look into adopting one from one of the many guide dog centers around the country. Today there are approximately 5,000 dogs working as guide dogs for the blind and thousands more being used to help handicapped people who are deaf, quadriplegic, paraplegic or suffering from such diseases as multiple sclerosis or spina bifida. As well as being loving companions, these dogs are the eyes and ears of their handicapped owners.

It takes a great deal of training for a dog to qualify for this work. They must be at ease in all types of living conditions such as heavy traffic, loud noises, crowded pedestrian areas and with other animals. Because the standards are so high for these dogs, as many as 50 percent are often rejected from a typical guide dog program and placed in an adopted home permanently.

The benefit of having such a dog is that they are AKC registered purebreds, usually German Shepherds, Golden Retrievers and Labrador Retrievers. And even though they did not complete the rigorous training program, they are all exceptionally well-behaved, already housebroken and intelligent. There is usually a long waiting list for these dogs, some-times up to two years. If you don't mind the delay, you can call one of the many guide dog centers around the country and ask to be included on their waiting list. Since the cost of training a guide dog and master team is nearly $20,000, most centers request a donation to help offset these enormous costs.

Puppy Raisers

You can also obtain a free guide dog puppy from these schools to raise for 18 months. Since the guide dogs have to be well socialized before being trained for handicap work once they become an adult, the pups cannot be raised in a kennel environment. For this reason, guide dog centers commonly seek volunteers (usually called "puppy raisers") to take in the puppies, provide them with love, care, basic discipline and lots of socialization. In fact, puppy raisers are encouraged to take their puppy with them wherever they go, including the market, office buildings, elevators and other public places.

The dog school first screens potential volunteers during an interview. If you qualify, you are taught some basic obedience training techniques. You must then sign a contract that clearly states that the guide center owns the dog and can take the puppy away if they feel it is being raised improperly.

You get to raise a purebred dog and, in many cases, receive a discount on expenses, especially medical needs. Perhaps the greatest benefit, though, is that if your dog doesn't pass the rigorous training program, you get first right of refusal on adopting the dog yourself. Of course, if your dog does qualify for handicap work, you must say good-bye. Many people find this volunteer work very rewarding, especially when they formally give the dog to its new handicapped owner upon the dog's graduation.

Look up guide dog schools at: www.rdcbraille.com/sourgd.html.

Guide Dog Centers

- Canine Companions for Independence www.caninecompanions.org. E-mail: info@caninecompanions.org. National Headquarters, PO Box 446, Santa Rosa CA 95402-0446; 800-572-2275.

- International Guiding Eyes, Inc. www.kitsap.net/services/gda. 13445 Glenoaks Blvd. Sylmar, CA 91342, 818-362-5834.

- Guide Dogs for the Blind www.guidedogs.com. PO Box 151200, San Rafael, California 94915-1200; 800-295-4050.

- Leader Dogs for the Blind www.leaderdog.org/main.html. Box 5000, Rochester, MI 48308, 888-777-5332.

- The Seeing Eye, Inc. www.seeingeye.org. PO Box 375, Morristown, N.J. 07963-0375, 973-539-4425.

- Guiding Eyes for the Blind, Inc. www.guiding-eyes.org. 611 Granite Springs Road Yorktown Heights, NY 10598, 800-942-0149.

- Pilot Dogs, Inc. www.pilotdogs.org. 625 West Town Street, Columbus, OH 43215; 614-221-6367.

- Canadian Guide Dogs for the Blind. PO Box 280 Manotick, Ontario, Canada KOA 2N0, 613-692-7777.

- The Seeing Eye www.seeingeye.org. 800-539-4425; 973-539-4425.

- Guide Dog Users, Inc. www.gdui.org. 888-858-1008.

Hearing Dog Resources

Delta Society/American Humane Association Hearing Dog Resource Center at www.petsforum.com/

deltasociety/dsd000.htm. E-mail: info@ deltasociety.
org, PO Box 1080, Renton, WA 98057, 800-869-6898.

Their service increases awareness and promotes
access rights for hearing dogs used by the deaf and
hard of hearing. They will send you a free copy of
their pamphlet, *Hearing Dog Fact Sheet*, which
explains what hearing dogs do, the cost involved
and how to obtain one. They will also send you a
free copy of their *Hearing Dog Training Center
Directory*, which lists hearing dog placement centers across the country.

Paws with a Cause Home of Ears for the Deaf,
Inc. www.pawswithacause.org. 4646 South Division,
Wayland, MI 49348, 800-253-PAWS (7297). Paws
with a Cause trains Assistance Dogs nationally for
people with disabilities and provides lifetime team
support which encourages independence. PAWS
promotes awareness through education and has
representatives throughout the U.S.

Dogs for the Deaf, Inc. www.dogsforthedeaf.org.
E-mail: info@dogsforthedeaf.org. 10175 Wheeler
Road, Central Point, OR 97502, 541-826-9220.
Their service enables hearing-impaired people to
use specially trained dogs as their "ears" to the
world, thereby giving them independence, freedom
and constant companionship. Dogs are chosen from
local animal shelters where they would otherwise

be put to sleep. Following four months of training during which time they are taught to alert their owners to such everyday sounds as an alarm clock, a smoke alarm, a doorbell, specialized phones and even a baby's cry, the dogs are matched to their owners. While the cost is $5,000 per dog, the service is provided free of charge to qualified applicants.

Pets Helping People

Just as there are groups that place older or retired pets, there are also programs, funded through government grants or private donations, that provide companion pets for seniors. Examples of these programs are:

Pets are Worth Saving www.ourinternet.com/paws/pawsindex.html or www.pawschicago.org/about_paws/index.html (has branches nationwide).

Progressive Animal Welfare Society www.paws.org. Lynwood, WA; 425-787-2500.

Representatives from these programs visit senior centers, retirement homes and retirement communities (accompanied by homeless pets) to help spread the word about their adoption services. Some programs even provide free veterinary services, cover the cost of neutering and supply transportation and food for those who can't afford the costs of owning a pet.

Pet Partners is a national registry of pets and volunteers who visit lonely, ill and disabled people. Pet Partners is offered by the Delta Society, an international non-profit organization that promotes beneficial relationships between animals and people. Visit their web site at: www.petsforum.com/DeltaSociety/dsa000.htm. Pet Partners include dogs, cats, birds and other pets. They accompany owners on visits to nursing homes, hospitals, schools, prisons, treatment centers and other facilities. For more information write: Pet Partners Program, Delta Society, 289 Perimeter Road East, Renton, WA 98055-1329, 800-869-6898, E-mail: info@deltasociety.org.

PAWS/LA www.pawsla.org/index.htm. 213-650-PAWS in Los Angeles; 415-824-4040, in San Francisco. Located in the Los Angeles area (there is also a program in San Francisco www.pawssf.org), this tax-exempt non-profit organization helps people with AIDS/ARC related disabilities keep their pets. This is one of the most compassionate, supportive services available. PAWS provides domestic pet care including walking, grooming, feeding and transportation to veterinary appointments. Their devoted volunteers find foster homes for pets when people with AIDS/ARC are hospitalized or unable to care for their pets. In addition, they provide pet food, supplies and assistance with acute care in emergency situations. They will also find permanent homes for pets, arranged in consultation with the owner who is given the opportunity to become acquainted with their pet's prospective new family.

Pet Owners with AIDS/ARC Resource Service Inc. (POWARS) www.powars.org e-mail: steve@powers. org.com. POWARS, Inc., PO Box 1116, Madison Square Station, New York, NY 10159. This organization helps people with AIDS care for their pets. Their services include dog walking, vet care, counseling, grooming and in-home foster care.

The Holistic Animal Consulting Centre, 29 Lyman Ave., Staten Island, NY 10305, 718-720-5548. They provide information on companion animals for people diagnosed with AIDS and stress the fact that, for some people with AIDS, animal companions represent the only relationship that remains unaltered by the diagnosis.

Adopting a Different Kind of Pet

In addition to dogs and cats, there are also horses, burros, rabbits, farm animals and even monkeys available for free adoption. When our daughter started horseback riding, we were able to obtain free, already-trained horses from a summer camp in exchange for feeding and giving them a home for the nine months of the year when they weren't being used by the camp. Later, she was given another good trail horse for free from a local resident who didn't have the time to ride anymore and wanted someone to exercise her horse and provide it with a good home. By keeping a lookout in the local papers, or even placing your own ad and asking neighborhood horse owners "to put the word out," there is a good chance that similar opportunities will present themselves.

The Bureau of Land Management (BLM) www.adoptahorse.blm.gov division of the federal government sponsors an "Adopt-a-Horse or Burro Program." The BLM is the agency responsible for managing the nation's herds of wild horses and burros. When the herds become too large for the range to support, some of the animals are rounded up and offered for adoption. More than 100,000 of them have been taken in by people. If you are interested in providing a home for a wild horse or burro write: Bureau of Land Management, Attn: Karen Malloy, 7450 Boston Blvd., Springfield, VA 22153, Phone: 800-370-3936 or e-mail: Karen_Malloy@es.blm.gov. Most burros are easily tamed and quickly adapt to ranch or rural backyard living.

The House Rabbit Society www.rabbit.org/ arranges adoptions of house rabbits. This is a national non-profit organization that arranges adoptions and distributes information on the care, feeding and health of rabbits. They also provide needy rabbits with food, housing, veterinary care and, eventually finds them permanent homes. House Rabbit Society rabbits are spayed or neutered, litterbox trained and socialized. The main office of the HRS is located at 1524 Benton Street, Alameda, CA 94501. There are a number of branch chapters and other umbrella organizations nationwide and in Canada. For links to these chapters go to: fig.cox.miami.edu/Faculty/Dana/hrs.html.

West Valley Wuzzels www.wuzzles.com/ferrets/ documents/whatisducksoup.htm has a rescue program and shelter for ferrets. Located in Phoenix, AZ. 602-547-0031.

Adopting Farm Animals

Are you interested in adopting a farm animal? There are also rescue groups that place sheep, goats, hens and so on with good homes. Go to the web site: fig.cox.miami.edu/Faculty/Dana/hrs.html which maintains links to a number of these organizations. Examples include:

Pasado's Safe Haven www.PasadoSafeHaven.org. PO Box 171 Sultan, WA 98294; Ph: 360-793-9393; E-mail: SusMichael@aol.com.

Farm Sanctuary www.FarmSanctuary.org. PO Box 1065 Orland, CA 95963, Phone: 530-865-4617,

E-mail: shelter@farmsanctuary.org. They operate a referral and placement services for abused and abandoned farm animals and participate in the Adopt-a-Farm-Animal program. They use direct activism, legal action, public education and lobbying to protect wildlife and fight cruelty to animals.

Simian Society of America www.simiansociety.org. E-mail: info@simiansociety.org. If your tastes run towards the more exotic, this is an adoption and relocation service for unwanted monkeys. They stress the complex needs and multitude of problems associated with keeping primates and discourage those who are not fully prepared for the experience. For those committed to providing captive primates with long-term, care-conducive homes, the SSA offers health, diet, psychological well-being and management information as well as access to a network of experienced primate caretakers.

Helping Hands www.helpinghandsmonkeys.org/criteria.htm. 514 Cambridge Avenue, Boston, MA 02134, 617-787-4419. Provides trained monkeys to disabled persons. They need foster homes to raise monkeys from six to eight weeks to three to four years of age. Foster families are reimbursed for medical care and are supplied with free food for the monkey.

Alpaca Locator Service www.alpacanet.com/. This site is dedicated to the large, furry pets that resemble llamas. View the upcoming alpaca cam. The site has a free service for locating alpacas: "The AlpacaFinder service is a free consultation service designed to help you in your search for the right alpaca(s) to meet your specific needs. All information is kept confidential and is used only for consultation purposes."

American Tortoise Rescue www.tortoise.com/. Adopt a tortoise through this site.

You can find free classified ads for pets, livestock, etc. at www.stormloader.com/garagesale/pets.htm.

The Horsemarket has free classified ads at www.thehorsemarket.com for those interested in buying or selling a horse.

PetExpo at www.pet-expo.com/petclass.htm offers free classified advertising for pets of all types.

The AnimalHome web site at www.AnimalHome.com is a search engine for people needing a home for a pet and for people searching for a pet.

Home Television Shopping for Pets

The recent craze in home video shopping has even branched into home pet shopping. One such show airs on cable television (KDOC-TV) in Long Beach, CA. Twice a week host Fred Bergendorff of "The Pet

Place"—www.otn.com/ThePetPlace/HomePage.html; E-mail: Tpetplace@aol.com-surrounds himself with a menagerie of barking, howling, panting, scratching, sniffing pets looking for good homes and human companionship. The pets are from local animal shelters who are desperate to place the hoards of pets they rescue. Since The Pet Place began airing, responses at the shelters have increased more than 50 percent. Elevad Productions, PO Box 16806, Irvine, CA 92623. 949-474-9510.

Petline www.wusatv9.com/petline9/petline.html, produced by WUSA-TV9, broadcasting from Washington, DC features animals for adoption from local shelters. The web site has numerous links to animal groups and shelters. E-mail: petdr@ wusatv9.com. 202-895-5999.

The PuppyCam Network www.thepuppycam. com features live webcam adoption networks utilizing the power of the Internet to help puppies and kittens in shelters around the country find homes. The site provides an index to featured Cam sites at shelters that participate.

A Final Word

Something you should know: pets from shelters and even those from pet shops have often received little, if any, recent health care and should have a thorough examination by a veterinarian within three days of purchase or adoption. Pets acquired through breeders run less risk of health problems. In most states if your new pet is found to be unhealthy, the law requires the seller to refund or exchange it for another. However, make sure to get a bill of sale with your animal so that the seller can't claim your payment as an adoption fee and get around the law.

Finally, if you're looking to adopt a pet, don't forget to check with local veterinarians, especially if there is no animal shelter in your area. Vets are frequently asked to put to sleep unwanted cats and dogs of all ages. Owners bring in healthy animals that they can't keep for a variety of reasons and for which they are unable to find homes. Vets are usually happy to give these animals away free so that they don't have to be put to sleep.

CHAPTER 2

Free Food, Treats & Toys for Your Pet . . . Plus Discounts and Savings for Fido and Fluffy

To his dog, every man is Napoleon; hence the constant popularity of dogs.

—Aldous Huxley

Easy $$—Coupon Your Way to Saving

How can we save money on the food, treats and toys we lavish on our beloved companions? The easiest way to save is as simple as reading your Sunday newspaper.

If you've ever glanced at the brightly colored coupon section of your Sunday newspaper, you know that coupons must be a big business. Why else would manufacturers spend millions of dollars advertising $.25 to $1.50 and more off their products? They want you to try their products and then become loyal, repeat customers.

Major supermarket brand pet food manufacturers advertise heavily in newspaper coupon sections. Luckily for us, theirs are among the most high-value coupons available. When you consider that many supermarkets double manufacturers coupons, you're talking about significant savings on your next purchase of dog or cat food. If you are not a brand-loyal shopper, you can use cents-off coupons nearly every time you shop. Many pets will gobble up any brand of food you give them and ask for more. They seem to thrive on whatever you put in front of them.

Some pets require special diets. Some like variety in their meals or a combination of canned and dry food. Most manufacturers today make several varieties of pet foods formulated for a pet's health and age. Coupons are almost always good for any size or formula of a manufacturer's product, so you can give your pet a specifically formulated diet and save money at the same time. Premium pet food manufacturers such as Iams, Science Diet and Nature's Recipe also offer savings on their products. You can find their coupons in the pages of pet magazines, newsletters and in pet stores that carry their brands. If you are interested in nutritional formulas or want more detailed information about a brand of food, write directly to the manufacturer and they will gladly send you lots of information about their products. In addition, nearly all companies will also include valuable discount coupons (without an expiration date) for use with your next purchase. These coupons are often worth several dollars off the retail price.

The following are examples of recently offered "cents-off" discounts for pet food products (remember, the value of these coupons are doubled at most supermarkets):

- 30¢ off any size Kitten Chow

- 60¢ off on 12 cans of Fancy Feast gourmet canned cat food

- 35¢ off one package of Milk-Bone dog biscuits or T.C. biscuits

- 35¢ off one package of Milk-Bone T.C. rawhide strips

- 50¢ off Lafeber's Nutri-Berries bird food

- 40¢ off any size Sunshine dog or cat food

- 30¢ off any size package of Frosty Paws

- 55¢ off any bag or two boxes of Friskies dry cat food

- 55¢ off on any size Friskies Kitten Formula dry kitten food

- 50¢ off on two bags of Lip Smackers (people cookies for dogs)

- $4 off a 7 lb. or larger size bag of any Nutrix brand pet food blend

- $2 off any size bag Pro Plan brand

- $1 off on 3.5 lb. Purina O.N.E. Optimum dog or cat formula

- $2 off any 20 or 40 lb. size Pro Pac dog or cat foods

- $2 off any Science Diet product with purchase of any size bag or six cans of any canine or feline Science Diet formula

- 50¢ off any 2 boxes of Pounce treats for cats

Free Food on Your Table and in Your Pet's Bowl
Nearly every week, along with "cents-off" coupons, there are dozens of offers for "free" products,

often groceries, with a purchase of a brand pet food. The following are examples of recent "Free with Purchase" coupon offers:

- Free can of Pedigree Choice Cuts when, you bought Pedigree Mealtime, 10 lb. bag or larger

- Free can of Grand Gourmet dog food (same size) when you bought three cans of Grand Gourmet, any size or variety

- Free Groceries (up to $1) when you bought any bag of Gaines Gravy Train

- Free groceries (up to $1.50) with purchase of any size Chuck Wagon Lean dog food

- Free groceries (up to $3) with purchase of 18 lb. or larger bag of Purina Kibbles and Chunks dog food

- Free can, same size, when you bought four cans of Mighty Dog canned dog food, any size or variety

- Free groceries (up to $1.50) when you bought one 3.5 lb. bag or larger of any variety Purina O.N.E. pet food

- Free groceries (up to $1.50) with purchase of any size Purina Gravy dog food

- Free groceries with purchase of any size Purina Kibbles and Chunks dog food

- Free can with purchase of three cans of Friskies Kitten Formula canned kitten food, any variety

- Free can of Pedigree Food for Puppies when you bought any size bag of Pedigree Food for Puppies

- Free package of Snausages sausage style snacks for dogs with purchase of any bag of Kibbles 'n Bits dog food

- Free groceries (up to $2) with purchase of any size Nature's Course dog food

- Free groceries (up to $3) with purchase of 20 lb, or larger Nature's Course dog food

- Free groceries (up to $1) with purchase of 5 lb. or larger Purina Hi Pro dog food

- Free groceries with purchase of any size bag of Come 'N Get It dry dog food

- Free groceries (up to $1) with the purchase of any size Purina Puppy Chow puppy food

- Free groceries (up to $2) with the purchase of 20 lb. or larger Purina Puppy Chow puppy food

- Free groceries (up to $1.50) with purchase of any 20 or 25 lb. bag of Gaines Cycle Adult dog food

- Free groceries (up to $1) with purchase of any 5 or 10 lb. bag of Gaines Cycle Adult dog food

- Free groceries when you bought two boxes or one bag, any size, of Alpo Gourmet dinner or seafood flavor cat food.

- Free groceries (up to 75¢) when you bought two boxes or one bag of new Alpo seafood flavor cat food

- Free groceries (up to $1) with purchase of one 4, 5, 9, 20 or 40 lb. bag of Purina Fit & Trim dog food

- Free 5 lbs. with every 50 lb. purchase of Omolene 100, 200 or 300 formula for horses

- Free trial size Purina O.N.E. brand pet food or 79¢ off any variety of O.N.E.

- Free can of cat food with the purchase of five cans (any size) of Alpo Cat Food.

The following offers had a place on the coupon to write your name and address for any additional money saving coupons and products by mail:

- Free can of 9 Lives Cat Food when you bought any ten cans

- Free can of Reward Dog Food when you bought two 3 oz. or one 6 oz. Jerky Treats dog snacks

- Free groceries (up to $1.50) with purchase of one 20 lb. bag or larger of Come 'N Get It dry dog food

- Free can Reward dog food with Meaty Bone brand dog biscuits

- Free can Skippy Premium with 4 cans of Skippy dog food

- Free can of Amore Gourmet cat food with two cans of Amore

- Two free cans of 9 Lives cat food with 9 Lives Crunch Meal

- Free Friskies Calendar with Proofs of Purchase

- Free Mighty Dog Calendar with Proofs of Purchase

More Discounts on Stuff for Your Pet

In addition to savings on pet food and groceries, there are discounts on a variety of pet-related supplies. Some recent offers included:

- $1 mail-in refund offer with proof of purchase from Shield flea and tick control

- Buy one, get one free, Ever Clean ES formula liquid waste remover for litter boxes

- $1 off any 48-pack Dispoz-A-Scoop disposable pooper scoopers

- 40¢ off on a 7 or 16 lb. jug of Scoop Away advanced cat litter

- 50¢ off on any size Fresh Step cat litter

- 50¢ off any box of Arm & Hammer Carpet deodorizer

- 25¢ off purchase of 5.5 lb. Super Sand cat litter

- 40¢ off on Purina Cat Chow self-feeder

- 25¢ off any Cardinal product (shampoo products for dogs)

- Buy two jugs of Super Sand, miracle cat litter at regular price and get one free

- 30¢ off purchase of any size Cat's Pride original cat litter

Also, look for mail-in refund and rebate offers (often advertised next to "cents-off" coupons) for pet food and supplies. These are usually good for cash refunds of $1 to $4 or more with proof of purchase.

Absolutely Free—Sample Goodies, Treats and More

These are the best. Free samples and trial size offers are available for every imaginable pet food, treat and goodie. Over the past year we have collected a small mountain of freebies that would fill most kitchen pantries. Where do they come from? Pet stores, pet shows, veterinary clinics, feed stores, spay and neuter clinics sponsored by pet food manufacturers, breeders and by contacting manufacturers directly. In most cases, all you have to do is walk in and ask for samples.

Many food samples are high-quality, scientifically formulated products recommended by veterinarians and breeders. With most animal professionals recommending that pets be fed a "life stage" diet, collecting samples and trying them is a great way to find out which kind agrees with your pet. Try different foods and food combinations. When you have found a healthy, balanced diet your pet likes, stick to it.

Check local markets and pet stores or feed stores for special offers. Manufacturers will often tie in with a local supplier to get customers to try their brand. In this case they will supply the pet store with free products and the store passes the free offer on to the public, either through a mailer or advertisement.

Example: One recent offer consisted of a free 5 lb. bag of dog food or a free 3 lb. bag of cat food. No other purchase was necessary. Along with a recent $3 off rebate offer, Science Diet gave special coupon-bearing customers a free trial-size bag of any Science Diet Formula for dogs or cats.

By far, the greatest amount of free samples are available at pet shows, pet and feed stores, and veterinary clinics. Most places will allow you to take generous helpings of the samples on display. After all, if your pet likes the freebies, they're hoping you will come back and buy more of their product. The following are some of the free samples we picked up during a couple of days of "shopping":

- Science Diet—Free Nutrition Kits that teach owners about preventive health care for their pets. Kits include a generous food sample, Health Record card, facts on our pet at his stage of life and a detailed guide to preventive health care. Science Diet makes kits for active adult dogs, puppies, kittens, older dogs, adult dogs, adult cats and overweight adult cats.

- Purina—Free trial size dog food samples of Purina Pro Plan Lite Formula, Adult Formula, Performance Formula, Growth Formula and trial size samples of Adult Formula cat food.

- Wysong Distributing—Free samples of junior Growth for dogs, Feline Vitality for cats and Adult Maintenance for dogs.

- 6-oz. sample cartons of Chunks for dogs, Less Active for dogs, Puppy Food, Mini Chunks for dogs, Cat Food and Less Active for cats.

- Eukanuba—Free 6 oz. samples of Eukanuba for Puppies, Eukanuba for dogs, Adult Eukanuba Maintenance for dogs and Growth Eukanuba for puppies.

- Nutro—Free samples of Max Special for senior, less active and overweight dogs; Max Cat lite for less active, neutered and spayed cats; Max kibble dog food for adult dogs; Natural Choice lamb and rice formula dog food; Max Puppy and Max Cat.

- Nature's Recipe—Free 4 and 6 oz. samples of Optimum Feline Diet Lite, Nonmeat kibble dog food, Lamb and Rice kibble dog food, Senior/ Pension dog food and Optimum Feline Diet.

- Breeder's Choice—Free samples of Complete wheat base dog food (trial size), Puppy Formula (trial size) and AVO-DERM dog food (for healthy skin and coats).

- Martin Techni—Cal-Free samples of Techni-Cal cat food (120 gms), Techni-Cal senior dog food (200 gms), Techni-Cal growth dog food (200 grams) and Techni-Cal mini maintenance dog food (200 grams.).

In addition, we also picked up these freebies:
- Starter dose of Pet—Tabs/F.A. for Dogs and Cats (vitamin granules and tablets) from Beecham Laboratories

- Complimentary first bath Mycodex Pet Shampoo

- Sample Dispoz-A-Scoop pooper scooper from Petpro Products

- Sample Flea Stop shampoo (1 fl. oz.) from Terminix

- A sample of "Cat Love," the happy, healthy cat treat from Hagen

- Trial size sample (6 oz.) of dog food chunks from Sunshine

- ½ lb. sample of the Abady dog food for maintenance and stress

- Waffle-shaped beef basted dog biscuits (2.2 oz.) from Wagtime

- Trial size sample of Lafeber's Nutri-Berries cockatiel food

- From Hikari, makers of fancy goldfish (koi) products: samples of wheat germ gold fish & koi food, cichlid Excel fish food wheat germ & spirulina formula, chiclid staple complete balanced nutrition fish food and Hikari excell color enhancing food for koi

- A 2 oz. sample of Aquatic Turtle Food and 2.5 oz. sample of Hermit Crab Food from Zoo Menu

- Samples of Arno Chlor, fresh water and marine water conditioner and Shieldex, fresh and marine water conditioner

- 50 oz. gm. sample of Swimny Premium Blend koi food from Nippon Pet Food Co.

Web Sites for Coupons, Freebies and Special Offers

Free Dog Food www.chicorybenefits.com/sample_form.htm. Receive a free sample of ALPO, ". . . the only canned dog food that contains whole chicory root, a highly effective and natural prebiotic that promotes your dog's digestion and overall health."

Animal Essentials www.animalessentials.com/samples.html has an online form to request samples of two of its supplements.

Aquatic Foods www.aquaticfoods.com/freesamples.html offers a gift certificate for a free sample of California Blackworms.

The Bird Crazy Mall www.birdcrazy.com/new.htm will accept e-mail requests for samples.

Breeder's Choice Pet Food www.breeders-choice.com/ provides an e-mail option for receiving coupons. Also offers an online form for joining the

Pinnacle Frequent Buyer program which enables participants to obtain a free bag of food with proof of purchase seals and a free gift.

Brisky Pet Products www.brisky.com/sample.html offers an online form to receive Accu Feed samples for ferrets, hedgehogs, sugar gliders and chinchillas. The online sample requires a $3.00 fee. All requests for free samples must be made through a toll-free telephone number (1-800-462-2464).

CoolSavings.com www109.coolsavings.com has coupons for pet products and other free stuff.

Coupon Exchange www.couponexchange.com offers free coupons to the consumer.

CouponSurfer.com www.couponsurfer.com/faq.cfm is a free Internet coupon service which you can personalize for pet related products. Coupons are both the online variety and printable coupons.

Cyberdog at cyberdog.com/samples.htm has an online form for free samples.

ePetVillage www.epetvillage.com has an online membership form. Offers savings on great pet products, pet friendly hotels, pet airline tickets, and much more.

Gaines web site www.gainespetfoods.com/samples.html has information on how to receive samples of Munchees, and Nuggets & Nibbles dog treats. Occasionally the samples are unavailable.

Hamilton Horse Cookie Company www.horsecookie.com offers an online form for a sample of Tally Oats.

Heartland Ranch www.geocities.com/Heartland/Ranch/1146/free.html will send a free sample of its dog biscuit.

Heinz at www.kibbles-n-bits.com/coupon.htm offers Kibbles-n-Bits coupons.

High Hopes Dog Food www.highhopes4pets.com/hh_free.html offers an online form for a free sample.

Hills Science Diet www.hillspet.com/stage/breeder4/association.html (800-654-5631) provides coupons and discounts to breeders who maintain three or more breeding dogs and register one litter a year. A store locator service for Hills Science Diet products is provided at 800-633-6357.

The Horse Candy Mall at www.horsecandy.com/sitemap.htm has extensive links to free games, puzzles, screensavers and information It has an online form to be put on a waiting list for a sample of its horse treats.

HOT Coupons www.hotcoupons.com is an online local coupon source for pet products.

Iams www.iams.com/register/index.asp has an online form that you can use to register for free petfood.

ILoveMyPet www.ilovemypet.com/news/coupons. html offers coupons for Neura and ANF dog and cat food.

Internet Coupon Directory www.coupondirectory. com has links to a variety of coupon web sites.

J.E. Ronicker Laboratories www.kittybloom. com will send a free sample of Xtrabloom Wate, a powdered fat for cats that aids weight gain, improves coats and makes food more palatable. If you are concerned whether your cat is getting enough vitamins and minerals, they will include a sample of Kitty Bloom VM900+2, an advanced formula cat supplement. Call them at 800-833-4748.

The Lafeber Company www.lafeber.com/main. html will send a trial size sample of its high quality bird food if you e-mail your name, street address, city, state, zip, phone and the type of bird you own to info@lafeber.com.

Mighty Dog dog food has a mail in offer at www.friskies.com/md/md_so_offer1.html.

MyCoupons www.mycoupons.com/codes/start. phtml lists free offers and coupons and discounts from a variety of online merchants. For example, PetSmart.com offers a free Toy Story 2 Woody toy with a $20 purchase.

National Pet Products www.natpetwi.com/natl. html occasionally has special offers for its dog food.

Nature's Recipe 1-800-237-3856 will send a coupon for a free can of dog or cat food and coupons for $4 off dry dog food; $3 off dry cat food.

Natural Life Pet Products uses no artificial preservatives, meat by-products, sugar or nitrates and nitrites. For a free sample of their formulated product (let them know if you have a dog or a cat), call them at 1-800-367-2391.

Nu Pro www.nuprosupplements.com/ferret_info. html offers a sample of its ferret supplement.

NutroMax (800-833-5330) will send a sample of their product, subject to availability.

PetExpress www.petxpress.com/petfood has ongoing offers. Recent offers included two for one Iams sale, 5% off Eagle products and $5 off on a $30 order.

Pet Food Direct's web site at www.petfooddirect.com/store offers include:
- $2.00 OFF 24/5.5-oz cans of Mighty Dog;
- $2.00 OFF 24/3.0-oz cans of Fancy Feast—all Varieties;
- 20% OFF all Kaytee Fiesta & Rainbow Exact Bird Foods;
- 20% OFF all JW Pet Company Dog and Cat Toys;
- free Pro Plan Canned Cat Food!

Power Paws www.powerpaws.com/free.htm will send a free sample of its product.

Presicutt Doggy Treats future.futureone.com/~stuff/page2.html offers a small bag of dog bisuits for $2.00.

Pro Pac Premium Dog Food www.propacpetfood.com has an online form to receive offers and coupons.

Purina has a treat offer at www.purina.com/treats/treatscat/whisker_lickins.html.

Purina offers special promotions at www.dog chow.com/special.html.

Purina's Fit and Trim web site www.fitandtrim.com/product_info/freeKit.htm offers a free weight loss kit.

Purina offers a free sample of cat and dog treats at offers.purina.com/guestbook/guestbook.asp?prog=treats.

Purina O.N.E. www.purinaone.com/frameset.asp?section=contest has a contest offering a year's supply of pet food.

Quick Coupons www.qpons.com offers e-mail sign up for notification when coupons are available in a consumer's region.

Rio Vista Products for horses and dogs www.riovistaproducts.com will send a free sample.

Royal Canine's web site at www.royalcanin.com/news.htm has a variety of free and coupon offers. Recent offers included a free 1-lb bag of Natural Blend Dogfood with coupon and a free 10-oz package of Sensible Choice dog treats with the purchase of an 18-lb bag or larger of dog food.

Select the Best www.selectthebest.com has an online form to request a free sample of its equine supplement.

TLC Premium Pet Food at www.petrix.com/$$$/sample.html offers a free sample.

3 Bears Dog Biscuits www.flyingdogpress.com/3bsample.html has an offer for a free sample; also an online form to enter drawing for free biscuits.

Treetwells www.treatwells.com/products/free.htm offers a free sample pack of Jokers Horse treets offers a free sample pack for $3.95 shipping and handling.

ValuePage www.supermarkets.com/Entry.pst is a coupon resource keyed to regional areas by zip code. Recent offers included coupons for Fancy Feast cat food and Alpo dog food.

Vita Treet www.vitatreat.com/coupons.htm has an online form for free coupons.

Watkins Pet Products www.watkinspet.com/mailform.html has an online form for a free sample and coupons.

Wow-Bow Distributors www.wow-bow.com has created a full line of health treats for pets. Hand cut and freshly baked, all their biscuits contain only the finest natural ingredients. Indicate whether you own a cat, dog or horse and they will send you a free sample of these nutritious, delicious biscuits. Write to: Wow-Bow Distributors, Ltd., 13-B Lucon Dr. Deer Park, New York 11729, info@bow-wow.com. Or call: 800-326-0230.

For those who like to do it themselves, free pet treat recipes can be found at:
- www.crl.com/~wizard/cook/frame.html
- expage.com/page/petrecipeindex
- soar.berkeley.edu/recipes/dog

Periodically check Value Page www.valupage.com/Entry.pst?From=KitchenLink for coupon offers and for savings on a variety of products. Recent rebate/free offers included:
- a free Mighty Dog Senior Pack which includes a collapsible travel food/water bowl; dog brush for a healthy, shiny coat; toothbrush for strong teeth and healthy gums; senior care brochure- an informative handbook on caring for your older dog; plus a money-saving coupon
- a free Friskies Millenium Scrapbook
- free Come 'n Get it Dog Food

If your cat is one that responds to the herb catnip, you will likely be able to find catnip plants or seeds at a nursery, garden center or greenhouse in your area. For a small initial investment you can grow enough catnip to make your own toys for your feline friend. Many mail order companies, such as Taylor's Herb Garden, 1535 Lone Oak Rd, Vista, CA 92084, (619) 727-3485, will send catnip seeds through the mail. Write or call for a catalog. Two online seed catalogs that offer catnip by mail order are:

- The GreenWeb Exotic Seed Company online catalog at www.boldweb.com/cgi-bin/extract
- Johnnyseeds at www.johnnyseeds.com

Brisky at www.brisky.com/sample.html has an online form at the Guestbook link to be entered into a free drawing and to receive promotional materials and special offers.

In addition to pet food samples, you can also receive samples of other pet-related products such as:

AAC Litterbox Liners www.angelfire.com/biz/liner4u offers a free sample for SASE.

American Absorbants Natural Products www.aanpi.com/coupons.htm offers coupons and rebates for Mother Earth Cat Litter for those living in selected states.

Arm & Hammer, the folks who have shown us the many uses of baking soda as a natural deodorizer, distribute samples of Pet Fresh, carpet & room deodorizing powder and air freshener to veterinary offices and clinics. Internet visitors to Arm & Hammer's web site www.superscoop.com/00/default.htm can get a coupon for a free box of Cat Litter Deodorizer-up to $2.29. Arm & Hammer also has a monthly "Cute Cat" contest, the winner of which receives a coupon for a free Arm & Hammer Super Scoop.

Free Cat Litter www.cedarfreshscoop.com/ques/index.html. Complete the online marketing survey and receive a coupon for free Cedar Fresh Cat Litter.

Free Cat or Dog Food www.highhopes4pets.com/hh_free.html. Fill out the online questionnaire and receive a free sample of High Hopes Dog Food or Cat Food.

Cedar Fresh Scoop www.cedarfreshscoop.com/ques/index.html offers a coupon for completing an online survey.

Creature Cookies hotyellow98.com/creature cookies/free.html will send a free birthday gift to your pet for $1 to cover costs.

Designer Pet Beds www.designerpetbeds.com/Winapetbed.htm has an online drawing to win a free pet bed.

DogToys.com store.yahoo.com/willie/index.html will send a free coupon book worth $250 with an order.

Dri-Dek interlocking floor tile www.dridek.com/noflash/industry/freesample.html keeps animals drier, cleaner and more comfortable in their cages, runs and pens. The cushioned tiles are also treated with antibacterial agents that help fight infection. For a free sample kit call 1-800-348-2398.

Little Wolf Industries www.littlewolf.com/cratepad.htm also distributes Dri-Dek pads and will send a free sample.

Feline Pine Cat Litter www.felinepine.com has a buy-one-get-one-free offer plus a coupon for a free 4 lb bag for filling in an online form. Also has a Breeder's Club with offers for cat breeders.

Finish Line Horse Products www.finishlinehorse.com/contact has an online form for a free catalog and product samples.

Flea Busters www.fleabuster.com/Games/survey.html offers a discount coupon for completion of an online survey.

Improve at www.stopitch.com/contact.html offers a sample of its product to correct dry skin problems in dogs.

Kitten Care Kit offers.purina.com/kittenchow/kitten_care1.asp. The site offers a kit to help you get started with your new kitten. You need to complete the online survey, and they will send you a free *Essential Kitten Care Kit* that includes: Coupon for Purina Kitten Chow; *Essential Kitten Care Booklet*; Pet Music CD (soothing music for your kitten while you're away); a Purina Kitten Chow magnetic photo frame.

Lactaid is a lactose reduced lowfat milk formula for humans who can't digest milk. Many vets also recommend it for cats who have a similar problem. The Lactaid lactase enzyme makes milk's lactose digestible. For a free sample call (800) LAC-TAID.

Life Serve.com at www.lifeserv.com/petserv has a free pet planning system that includes software and a Web-CD.

Noah's Pets Supplies www.noahspets.com. The site offers free shipping on orders over $30. The online catalog contains a wide variety of products including "Anti-Bark Devices," "Ultra-Sonic Fogger for Terrariums," and the "Drink well Pet Fountain."

Litter Box Liners www.angelfire.com/biz/liner4u/index.html. Offers heavy-duty litter box liners. Try a free sample before ordering by sending a self addressed #10 envelope with $.55 postage to AAC.

PetExtras store.yahoo.com/petextras/senfrienbon.html is sending out coupon books with great offers from over 20 pet related online stores. Normally these coupon books are available for $2.95 through PetSaverCoupons.com. It also has several online contests including an online form for a dog or cat treat drawing at www.petextras.com/petextras/catherhaphou.html.

Petfood express petfoodexpress.com/free_gift.asp has a free gift offer.

Pet Labels.com www.petlabels.com/free_sample.htm offers a free sample of its pet address label.

Pet Shopping Mall www.petshoppingmall.com/. This online retailer offers a free "surprise" with every order.

Pet Vitamins www.animalessentials.com/samples.html. The site offers free samples of vitamins for dogs and cats.

Planet Urine planeturine.com offers a free blacklight, which shows pet urine stains in carpet which may not be visible in normal light, with the purchase of its pet urine cleaning system.

Poop-off www.birdcrazy.com/mall/PoopOff.asp. 4-oz free sample offered with any order.

Purina www.purina.com/dogs/weight offers a free dog weight chart as part of their Fit 'n Trim promotion.

St. Hubert's Animal Welfare Center www.sthuberts. org/scoop/guest.htm has an online form for a free decal informing emergency personnel that there is a pet indoors.

Summit Flexible Products www.summitflex. com is the maker of high quality rubber mats for horses. Call them at 800-STALMAT for a sample of their shock block protector stall mat.

The Doggy Bag has a free sample at www.doggy-bag.com/. This is a product designed for dog owners to easily clean up after their dog.

The LaFeber Company www.lafeber.com/docs_book has an online book on pet birds.

Yesterday's News www.yesterdaysnews.com/products/productinfo.html has an online form for product information and free coupons.

Zuke's Power Bones Products has an online offer for a free doggy bandana with any purchase online www.zukes.com/promo.html.

Pet Warehouse at petswarehouse.com/petaquaria.htm has an online Aquarium of the Month contest. Winner of drawing wins $50.

Weight Loss Kit offers.purina.com/guestbook/promosplash.asp?prog=weightkit. Free "Fit & Trim" pet weight loss kit from Purina.

Web Sites—Pet Stuff Just for Fun

Pet Stories www.baddogs.com/. At this site, users can read others' stories about their pets for free, or submit their own story. "The Bad Dog Chronicles let Fido and Fifi share their misdeeds with other Net-connected canines and their masters. If you've ever had a furry doggie member of the family that's caused a ruckus or wrecked your belongings, you will have loads of fun reading about other owners' plights. Plus, you (or your dog) can add your own story, complete with damage total and a friendly reply from the four-footed."

A free dog screensaver at <u>hometown.aol.com/ bunnybrat6/dogchaser.html</u>.

Free pet cyber cards at <u>rats2u.com/calendar_opqr/ calendar_pets.htm</u>.

The Chazhound web site <u>www.chazhound.com/ petgames.html</u> has free pet games and screensavers.

Best Dog Free Stuff <u>www.workingdogweb. com/FreeStuff.htm</u> has games.

Cat Fanciers <u>www.fanciers.com/</u>. This site offers an extensive listing of resources for cat owners, including a directory of rescues and shelters, directories of information organized by breed, databases of cat shows and cat registries.

Famous Pets Index <u>www.citizenlunchbox.com/ famous/animals.html</u>. Originally designed as a guide for naming one's pets, the indexes of famous animals have grown into a pretty hefty reference database, boasting over 4,000 names.

Virtual Cat or Dog <u>www.virtualkitty.com/</u>. Create your own virtual cat or dog. Set a default Web page and when you click the "Emergency" button while playing with your pet, the Web page will appear.

This is useful to virtual owners who want to play with their pet at work.

Pet Market www.petmarket.com/. Free pet postcards from this colorful, well-designed online retailer site.

Petopia at www.petopia.com/register.asp?tab=0& subtab=0 has a free pet picture frame.

Online Pet Clubs www.kennelvet.com/. Join one of the free online pet clubs to discuss issues regarding pets with other pet owners and online experts.

Exotic Tropicals www.exotictropicals.com/. This site offers free animal care guides, including guides for small animal pets such as: Rabbits, Hamsters, Guinea Pigs, Rats, Mice, Chinchillas, Ferrets, Gerbils, Hedgehogs, Sugargliders, Prairie Dogs and more.

Potbellied Pig Association www.mindspring.com/ ~porcelainpig/pigbooks.htm. Through this site, there is a free service from the Potbellied Pig Association, which works to link prospective pig owners with lost or unwanted pigs.

Gerbils Home Page www.gerbils.org/. Free online community to discuss gerbils.

The Snake www.thesnake.org/. Free electronic cards with pictures of snakes, scorpions, lizards, alligators and more.

Frogs allaboutfrogs.org/froglnd.shtml. Free frog software, screensavers, cursors and icons at this site devoted to frogs.

Turtles www.crosswinds.net/~theturtlepages/software/index.html. Free turtle cursors and icons.

Guinea Pigs www.caviesgalore.com/. The site offers permanent, free, web-based e-mail. You can get screen names, and 4 Megs of space for all your messages. Set up filters and folders as well as signatures to personalize your e-mail.

Mice and Rats.com www.miceandrats.com/. Fancy mice exhibited in Great Britain. Not very useful. We just liked the web address.

Snail Cam www.wallybillingham.com/snail/. This Web Cam is of the site editor's personal snails. The picture is very clear, but don't wait for it to move.

Free Pirana hometown.aol.com/piranhahut/sale.html. Current owner wishes to give away two pirana fish (the site claims the fish are vegetarians).

Chinchilla Classified Ads <u>chinchilla-exchange.</u> <u>hypermart.net/welcome.html</u>. Free classified ads offering sale of chinchillas and related products and services.

Rabbit Web Cards <u>www.showbunny.com/gallery.</u> <u>htm</u>. Send an electronic greeting card featuring a cute rabbit picture.

Rabbitweb <u>www.rabbitweb.net/</u>. This site has free classified ads offering rabbits, rabbit-related services and rabbit products.

Exotic Birds <u>www.birdsnways.com/</u>. Variety of resources on exotic birds, including forums where bird owners can ask experts for advice. Also includes a free database where prospective bird owners can search for birds for sale by: Name-of breeder, store or advertiser on the Net; species or subspecies-examples: macaws, umbrellas, amazons, greys, pied; type of source-breeder, or store or private (classified); state or area code; age and type of birds wanted-examples: babies, breeding, older and breeders who ship. A recipe exchange lists recipes for homemade bird food.

Hawaiian Pet Names <u>www.hisurf.com/hawaiian/</u> <u>petnames.html</u>. Free database of names. Enter your pet's name and receive the Hawaiian equivalent.

Free Animal Screensaver files.webshots.com/ direct/general/direct.html. When you download and install the Webshots Desktop software, you get access to our popular Web shots Daily web site. The full-service "portal" site allows Web shots Desktop users to come online everyday to pick up the free Daily Photo.

Dog Art www.cs.umanitoba.ca/~djc/wiener/. A Far Side Collection by Gary Larson, these online paintings will make anyone laugh. The home page begins "Although seldom discussed in the writings of most art historians, the wiener dog (or dachshund, as at least twelve people still insist on calling it) was intermittently a favorite subject of many artists, including several of the Great Masters (although this remains controversial). In fact, throughout the history of mankind, the wiener dog has often been utilized as a symbol for many of our human traits: love, war, hunger, greed, fear, hypochondria, and swollen glands, to name just a few of the more common ones."

Free Portrait Postcards www.petsinpastel.com/ main.htm. This site is managed by the artist who paints the pet portraits. She offers several favorite pet portraits in the form of electronic postcards for no charge.

Free Pet Web Page burnerkitty.com/index.htm. Burner Kitty offers custom Web pages for pets, as designed by their owners.

In the Company of Dogs www.inthecompanyof dogs.com/aardvark. The site offers free web cards with a photo of a dog, selected from their collection of dog photos. The site also offers DOGe-mail a "free service to remind you to celebrate the birthday of that special dog or dogs in your life."

Animal Planet animal.discovery.com/. Sponsored by the Discovery Channel, this site offers free animal e-cards and an extensive list of animal Web Cams. Check out the puppy cam or the seal cam.

Pet Channel www.thepetchannel.com/. This site has free original pet cartoons. The Pet Fun section contains recreational diversions for pet enthusiasts. You can read funny pet stories from Pet Channel users, submit stories of your own, or view the pet gallery where you can send a picture of your pet. The Pet Channel also brings you the syndicated comic strip Citizen Dog. In the "Training" section, Pet Channel has compiled a variety of trainers specializing in Dog, Cat and Equine training.

Cyberpet www.cyberpet.com/. Visit this site just for the amazing graphics and the sense of humor exhibited by the editors. There is a long list of free resources, including The Breeders Showcase, which allows you to find K-9 Breeders around the world. Look for specific breeds in the alphabetical directory.

Free Kids Games and Free Puppies www. puppyzone.on.ca/index.html. Puppy Zone offers regularly updated online puppy pictures for kids to color and online puppy-related games. Puppy Zone also has a page dedicated to puppies that are free to a good home. The site also has a page dedicated to free training tips.

Online Cat Postcards www.crazyforkitties.com/. This site offers free online postcards with an original cat photo. The electronic postcards can be personalized and sent to the receiver of your choice.

Free Canineworld Services www.canineworld. com/freeservices.html. CanineWorld offers a long list of free services, including: free Web site hosting, free eshops, auctions, free group and personal organizer, and free Web-based meeting center for real-time collaboration, including sharing and viewing documents.

Bird Selection Guide www.poozleanimus.com/. Free online international database of birds and aviaries.

PetJam www.petjam.com/. PetJam offers free web sites, free e-mail and free digital postcards with pet photos.

Holistic Pet Care www.halopets.com/holistic.htm. Send your name and address to the address listed and the site editors will send you a free *Holistic Pet Care* book.

Virtual Pet freeseek.net/globalpets/index.html. This site offers virtual pets. The software, "Global Pets '98 is an advanced virtual pet program made for Windows 95, 98, or NT. In Global Pets your goal is to take care of your virtual pet, feed it, play with it, and watch it grow. You must keep it alive, and put it to bed, just as you would a real pet. You can even load other pets from our shelter!!"

Dating Service for Pet Lovers www.petloversunite.com/. The service offers one free month with purchase of membership plan. This is a unique service for bringing Pet lovers together with others who have something in common right from the start. The creators are pet lovers and decided it is difficult for people to meet their two legged mates, so Pet Lovers Unite Inc. was researched and developed.

Pet Search Engine www.thepetsearchengine.com/. The site offers a multitude of search capabilities for pet-related products and services. The site also offers: a free dating service for pet lovers that will be provided for surfers and single business owners to find pen-pals, friendship, dating or marriage; a pet of the month/grand prize and pet of the year contest as well as a free e-mail service.

Virtual Dog Park www.doggiefun.com/pets.shtml. Submit photos and a bio on your pet for entry into the virtual dog park. Site users rate the dogs and the winners receive a cash prize.

Canine Games www.caninegames.com/. Dedicated to Canine Games events, the site also offers free electronic cards, free e-mail, recipes and a free directory of dog parks across the U.S., organized by state. The site also contains a photo directory of missing dogs.

Pet Station www.petstation.com/. This site, which bills itself as the "Internet Home Base for People Who Love Pets," offers a variety of resources, including pet adoption services and a "Pets Bill of Rights."

Fish Link Central www.fishlinkcentral.com/. This site contains a variety of resources related to fish, including free software, icons and graphics, free e-zines, free expert advice, and free online fish postcards.

Horse Care Products www.farnam.com/. Free online "Horse Care Record Form." Free shipping on some products such as horse care videos. Rebates and coupons on other products.

Pet Loves Products www.petloves.com/. Free digital postcards with pet themes, over 1000 cards available, including music.

Horse Treat Recipes www.geocities.com/Heartland/ Ridge/2194/treats.htm. This site offers recipes for horse treats.

Pals 101 paloves.homestead.com/links.html. This site offers a wide variety of pet resources, including a free pet web site, pet adoption, pet stories and more.

Pet Gumball Machine www.antiquegumball.com/ index.htm. This online retailer offers free shipping on this machine that holds dry pet foods. The Gumball machine is specially designed so pets can work it by themselves www.antiquegumball.com/pet/.

Toll-Free Numbers for Coupons,
Samples and Information:

- Friskies Petcare Company: 800-258-6719

- Heinz Pet Products: 800-252-7022

• Hill's Pet Nutrition Line: 800-445-5777

• The IAMS Company: 800-525-4267

• Kal Kan Foods, Inc.: 800-525-5273

• Pet-AG: 800-323-0877

• The Quaker Oats Company: 800-4MY-PETS

Other Offers
• Alpo: 888-444-2576 Frisbee Training Manual for Dogs with over $4.00 in Coupons

• Canine Principle: 800-705-2111 Free 8 oz sample of "Canine Principle" Dog Food (in *Cat Fancy*)

• Cat Watch: 800-829-8893 Free Issue of "Cat Watch" — The Newsletter for Cat People (in *Cat Fancy*)

• Feeding Horses: 800-227-8941 Free Booklet "A Complete Guide to Feeding Adult Horses" from Purina

• Feline Principle: 800-705-2111 Free 8 oz sample of "Feline Principle" Cat Food (in *Cat Fancy*)

- Fish Are Fun: 800-526-0650 Free "Fish Are Fun" Informative Booklet from Tetra Pet Products (30 pg)

- Life Source: 800-211-9180 Free sample of "Life Source" Health Food for Cats and Dogs (in *Dog Fancy*)

- Nuture: 800-705-2111 Free sample of "Nurture" Veterinarian Style Dog Food (in *Dog Fancy*)

- Pet Owner's Supplement and Remedies Guide free from Dancing Paws: 888-644-7297

- Pet Products Plus: 800-592-6687 Free sample of Pet Products Plus Cat Food (in *Cat Fancy*)

- Pet Products Plus: 800-592-6687 Free sample of Pet Products Plus Dog Food (in *Dog Fancy*)

- Pet Scoop Video: 800-738-2880 Free Video on the "Pet Scoop" Portable Scooper (from Pet Star web site)

- Pet Training Video: 800-793-6510 Free Video from Radio Systems on Pet Training Systems

- Pure Breath Freshener for Pets: Samples and coupons by sending SASE to 31280 Oak Crest Dr., #1 Westlake Village, CA 91361

- Purina Cat Chow Coupon & Literature: 800-CAT-CARE

- Purina O.N.E: 800-787-0078 (x2031) Free sample of Purina O.N.E. Real Chicken Formula Cat Food

- Purina O.N.E: 800-787-0078 (x2025) Free sample of Purina O.N.E. Reduced Calorie Formula Dog Food

- Purina O.N.E: 800-787-0078 (x43) Free sample of Purina O.N.E. Reduced Calorie Formula Dog Food

- Purina O.N.E: 800-348-4700 Free sample of Purina O.N.E. Cat and Dog Food (they send one of each)

- Purina O.N.E: 800-204-1818 Free sample of Purina O.N.E. Cat and Dog Food (they send one of each)

- Purina O.N.E: 800-787-0078 (x0046) Free sample of Purina O.N.E. Beef and Rice Dog Food and Coupons

- Purina O.N.E: 800-787-0078 (x0045) Free sample of Purina O.N.E. Cat Food (coupons sent with sample)

- Purina O.N.E: 800-787-0078 (x40) Free sample of Purina O.N.E. Dog Food (coupons sent with sample)

- Purina O.N.E: 800-787-0078 (x42) Free sample of Purina O.N.E. Dog Food (coupons sent with sample)

- Purina Pro-Plan: 800-458-7755 Free sample of Purina Pro-Plan Cat and Dog Food (they send one of each)

- Purina Pro-Plan: 800-650-1991 Free sample of Purina Pro-Plan Cat and Dog Food (they send one of each)

- Purina Pro-Plan: 800-433-0500 Free sample of Purina Pro-Plan Pet Food for Cats, Dogs or Puppies

- ProPlan ProClub: 800-851-3148 Free "ProPlan ProClub" (Cat Breeders of 5+) Rebates/ Special Offers

- ProPlan ProClub: 800-851-3148 Free "ProPlan ProClub" (Dog Breeders of 5+) Rebates/Special Offers

- Purina Puppy Chow: 800-956-0899 Free sample of Purina Puppy Chow and Money Saving Coupon

- Sojourner Farms: 888-867-6567 Pet Food Mix Sample

- Trading Faces: 800-227-3101 Free Pet Trading Cards sample from "Trading Faces" (in *Dog Fancy*)

CHAPTER 3

Free and Low-Cost Health Care Services for Your Pet

Never try to out-stubborn a cat.
—Robert A. Heinlein

Most pets probably feel the same way we do about going to the doctor. Neither of us like it and we try to avoid it whenever possible. I know that as soon as I put one foot in the veterinarian's office, my dogs put on the skids, big time, and run the other way.

In addition to our mutual feelings of "What Am I Doing Here?" and "I Should Be Outside Playing," few of us love paying those rising medical costs, for either ourselves or our pets. Of course, there's medical insurance for us (although still a costly expense) and there's also medical insurance for our pets (a more reasonably priced alternative).

There are also several other money-saving alternatives when it comes to health care for our pets, especially for the most common treatments and preventative medical care that insures our pets stay happy and healthy. These include spay and neuter services, health exams, and evaluations and vaccination clinics.

Do the Right Thing: Control Pet Overpopulation

Pet overpopulation is an enormous problem that can only be solved and brought under control by spaying and neutering your pets. Every five minutes another 250 dogs and cats are born (that translates to almost 3,000 dogs and cats born every hour, compared to 400 human births an hour). In the U.S. alone, more than 15 million animals are brought into municipal and private animal shelters each year. Many of these animals are strays or abandoned, brought in by animal control officers or concerned citizens. Others are brought in by their owners who, for a variety of reasons, are unable to keep them. It is impossible for these overcrowded, overburdened shelters to find homes for all of them. As a result, nearly 70 percent, almost 11 million dogs and cats, puppies and kittens, must be destroyed because no one wants them. In addition, over $500 million in taxpayer money is spent to fund this unfortunate cycle.

The best way to reduce the number of pets that are being destroyed is to reduce the number of puppies and kittens being born. There are also other benefits to spaying and neutering your pets including:

- Your pet will be a more content, lovable family member.

- Your pet will be healthier, saving you money and resulting in a longer life for your pet.

- Your pet will stay closer to home, avoiding injury due to traffic accidents or fights with other animals.

- Your pet will not be frustrated by biological drives to reproduce.

- Your pet will be better behaved.

- In some areas, your pet's license will cost at least 50 percent less.

- You won't have to find homes for your pet's offspring.

Although veterinary costs are rising an estimated 1% per month, spay/neutering procedures are available at affordable rates. Due to the widespread support and encouragement from humane educators, S.P.C.A.s and humane societies, veterinarians, animal shelter workers, ethical dog and cat breeders and informed pet owners, low-cost surgeries have become available nearly everywhere.

Free clinics for qualified senior citizens and low income individuals are sponsored by most city or county Animal Regulation and Animal Care and Control departments. Public shelters and pounds also give rebates and refunds to people who adopt animals and then come back with their adoption receipts and sterility certificates proving that they've had their pet altered.

Friends of Animals web site www.enviroweb. org/foa/spaying/sp1.htm lists a spay/neuter hotline: 800-321-7387 and will send a list of veterinarians in your area and a certificate for 50% off the cost of a spay/neuter

SPAY/USA at www.spayusa.org is a national referral service for the public regarding low cost spay/neuter programs. By calling their toll-free number, 800-248-SPAY, you will receive information about the nearest low-cost program and will be sent a certificate as proof you have gone through the SPAY/USA network. It has over 900 programs and clinics nationwide with about 7,500 top-notch veterinarians in the network.

Free Spaying or Neutering petlovers101.com/. With their "Sponsor a Spay" Program, Pets 101 offers assistance to those who cannot afford the costs of spaying or neutering

Humane Societies, S.P.C.A.'s and hundreds of other non-profit groups nationwide offer periodic low cost clinics to pet owners. Some pet stores (Example: Petco) and veterinary hospitals also team up to offer low cost spay/neutering services. Many local non-profit groups offer certificate/coupon/ rebate programs with participating vets who discount their regular spay/neuter services. Check local newspapers for announcements and Community Calendar segments on local TV and radio broadcasts.

A sampling of web sites sponsored by regional humane societies that offer low-cost spay and neuter procedures:

- Georgia: Humane Services of Metro Atlanta www.hsma-atl.org/orderfrm.htm offers low cost spay-neuter certificates.

- Texas: This web site ccwf.cc.utexas.edu/ ~ifpc203/neuter.html lists various spay/neuter programs in North and Central Texas plus links to national programs.

- Washington State: The PAWS web site at <u>www.paws.org/shelter/resources/spayneuter</u> lists spay and neuter resources in the Puget Sound area.

- California: The San Francisco Humane Society <u>www.sfspca.org/spay.html</u> offers free spay and neuter clinics for homeless, free spay/neuter surgery for pets owned by San Francisco residents age 65 and older, free spay/neuter surgery for dogs and cats owned by homeless residents, free spay/neuter surgery prior to adoption for all sexually mature shelter animals; low cost (lowest in region) spay/neuter surgery for dogs owned by residents and low cost spay/neuter surgery for cats from outside San Francisco.

Keeping Fido and Fluffy Healthy—for Free

Many times pets from shelters have received little, if any, recent health care. Even if you buy your pet from a pet store or reputable breeder, there may be no guarantee that it is healthy and free from disease or internal problems. Most vets recommend having your new pet examined thoroughly within two to three days of purchase or adoption, and some suggest bringing your new pet in within 24 hours of adoption.

Many veterinary clinics offer a free "new pet" exam with proof of adoption from a licensed shelter, humane society or adoption agency. Check your local veterinary clinic about their free health exam policy. The regular charge for a complete exam and evaluation generally costs between $30 and $45.

Web sites with offers of free or low-cost vet exams:

- Bayside Queens Veterinary Hospital in New York offers a coupon at its web site www. baysidequeens.com/bvc for a free physical exam.

- Minnesota Valley Humane Society mnvalley.pair. com/vetslist.htm posts a list of veterinarians who will give free exams for just adopted animals

Low-Cost Vaccination Clinics

Low-cost vaccination clinics are one of the easiest, most convenient money-saving opportunities you can find. Keeping your pets' vaccines and annual boosters current is essential to protect them from dangerous pet diseases. There are no less than five routine vaccines needed by dogs and four for cats including rabies, 6-in-1 (dogs), 4-in-1 (cats), parvo, corona virus, bordetella, feline leukemia, chlamydia, distemper and tests and treatments for heartworms, tapeworms and roundworms. Individually, these vaccines and tests can cost up to $30 each.

Luckily, there are a number of ways to save on these costly but necessary health measures. Recognizing the fact that many people cannot afford the regular cost of vaccinations (and, therefore thousands of pets might run the risks of carrying and spreading potentially deadly diseases), some private veterinarians offer special low-cost vaccine clinics on a weekly or monthly basis. These are usually held on weekends or evenings when they won't interfere with regular office hours.

Your city or county Department of Animal Regulation and Control or local Humane Society may offer free or low cost clinics at local parks, community centers or pet stores.

Pet Prevent-a-Care www.18884dogcat.com is a specialized company that offers low-cost vaccinations for dogs and cats through their mobile clinics. Over 400 clinics a month are held in pet stores, farm supply stores and other locations in California, Oregon and Washington. Their web site contains an online form for e-mail information. Most clinics are held Saturdays and Sundays and some evenings. Vaccinations are performed by state-licensed veterinarians and written certification is provided to each pet owner. To find a clinic in your area call 1-888-436-4228.

VIP Vaccine Service www.vipvaccine.com/clinics. html has clinics in over 200 locations year round in the central/northern California area (1-800-HAPY-PET).

By taking advantage of these special services, you can save up to 60 percent off the regular price for a series of pet vaccines. In order to make the public aware of these clinics, pet stores, hospitals and public agencies advertise their dates and times in local newspapers.

You can also call your vet or nearby pet supply store for the date of the next scheduled low-cost clinic.

Vet Care Vaccination Services www.mobilepet care.com/index.html provides low-cost mobile vaccination clinics in the Southern California area. Their web site posts a monthly schedule of clinic locations.

PetService.com maintains a vaccination clinic locator at its web site www.petservice.com/vaxlocF.html.

In some areas pet owners can purchase vaccines for some canine and feline diseases at the local feed store or veterinary supply store and administer the vaccines themselves for a fraction of the cost of a trip to the vet.

PetMeds web site at www.petmeds.com/index. htm offers pet prescription medications at discount prices and has an online prescription form for use by your vet.

Free Internet Information on Pet Health

There are numerous web sites that feature free consultations with veterinarians in the form of FAQs and general health information. Some, such as www.catsunited.com, have online forms upon which questions can be submitted. Others offer free periodic e-mail newsletters, and online articles on animal health. Tufts University School of Veterinary Medicine, for example, offers a free preview issue of its monthly newsletter "Catnip" focusing on the health and well being of cats at its web site www.vec.tufts.edu/vetgeneral/newsletters/morecatnip.html.

The General Veterinary Hospital is your site for free monthly articles and for a pet owner to write and get a response by an expert www.ilovemypet.com/bjackson.html.

National Animal Poison Control www.napcc.aspca.org/. The ASPCA National Animal Poison Control Center is dedicated to providing the most medically useful veterinary poison and drug information possible. Veterinary health professionals provide the service, supported by a wide variety of other professionals committed to the same goals.

For articles and information about diseases and keeping healthy dogs and cats visit www.companionvets.com/links.htm.

Pet Medical Record www.rxdata.net/Pets/pethome. asp is a free site that allows you and your pet's records to be kept for medical personnel worldwide.

Protect your cat against rabies. Visit locutus. mes.umn.edu/Documents/B/B/BB492.html or www. catndoghospital.com/cathealt.htm for information about vaccination for your cats or kittens.

All Creatures Veterinary Clinic www.allcreatures. com/ offers online consultations starting at $9.95 but also has free information and links to general pet care information.

Information about a free 24-hour a day Ani-Med hotline is at www.huntingretriever.com/aspca_health. htm. Sponsors of the services will also send $5 worth of pet care coupons to callers.

What should you know about infectious diseases in cats? Go to dmoz.org/Recreation/Pets/Cats/ Health/Conditions and Diseases/ (it offers various links to articles about the diseases).

Did you know that February is Pet Dental Month? Go to www.sancarlosvet.com/AskTheDoc/Dental Month.html to learn more about pet dental problems and visit the link provided to Hills Company for products that lessen plaque. Also visit this great site for the FAQ's about pet bad breath and serious dental problems: www.woofs.org/health/dental/.

Learn about allergy relief from The Bramton Company on their homepage at www.bramton.com/. For more about allergy relief go to www.pet-expo. com/allergy.htm as a great source.

Learn Important Facts about Flea & Tick Control from Farnam Pet Products at biofleahalt.com/ new_products/new_products_archive.html.

Virtual Ferret Clinic www.ferretnews.org/clinic. html. In this Virtual Ferret Clinic, you will find a variety of health care issues related to the domestic ferret. All the information is provided courtesy of: Steven M. Sanders, D.V.M., Ruth Adams D.V.M., and Suzanne Lee D.V.M.

The American Veterinary Medical Association web site www.avma.org/care4pets.html has extensive online information on animal health, including "Animal Illnesses and Diseases" and "Information on Dental Care, Pet Population Control Vaccinations and More." The AVMA also operates 888/VetsHelp, a toll-free, fully automated pet health line.

Pet Massage www.debonosense.com. If you or your animal friend suffer from aches and pains, stiffness or stress, this site can offer a solution. The editor/masseuse can teach you specific bodywork techniques to improve the movement and comfort of your dog, cat, horse or yourself. Visit this site for information on relaxation through pet massage.

Aquarium Diagnosis Service www.pawprints. com/fish/. Enter basic information into the online form about your fish and their aquatic environment and receive a free report from Ralph Van Blarcom F.D.D. Fish Disease Diagnostician.

Pond Keeping aquasearch.net/pondkeeper/. The site has extensive resources on fish, ponds, water gardens, aquatic environments, and other resources. The site includes links to free fish e-zines.

Fish Diagnostic Advice www.actwin.com/fish/ disease/chart1.php. This diagnostic tool walks the fish owner through a series of environmental factors and fish anatomy (assisted by a large drawing of a fish with labeled anatomy) in order to diagnose fish diseases and ailments.

HomeVet at www.homevet.com/index.html is another veterinary web site.

Dr. Jim Humphries at www.dvmedia.com/vet clinic.html has "virtual clinics" for dog and cat owners.

Kennel Vet at www.KennelVet.com is a pet solution site which fosters collaboration and discussion about pet remedies and the products that help.

Alternative Veterinary Medicine altvetmed.com/. This site is sponsored by several veterinarians who practice alternative medicine. The site offers a wealth of information on their approach, including articles on specific pet ailments such as cancer and arthritis.

Waltham University www.waltham.com. The University's veterinary school provides extensive resources on animal health from the scientific and medical point of view.

Free Veterinarian Advice www.petz.co.uk/vetontheweb/new/. A veterinarian surgeon based in the United Kingdom offers free advice through this site. A pet owner can fill out the online form and anticipate his response by e-mail as soon as possible.

Free Veterinarian Advice www.homevet.com/. No-Fee consultation. Veterinarian Dr. Jeff offers a free initial consultation on pet ailments.

Free Veterinarian Advice www.veterinarymall.com/. At this page, www.veterinarymall.com/askthevet.html, there is a long list of veterinarians and veterinary hospitals that are available for questions.

Free Veterinarian Advice www.vetcentric.com/. This site is dedicated to providing free advice to pet owners regarding the health of their animals. Pet owners can search an extensive database of questions answered by veterinarians. Pet owners can also submit a question to a veterinarian regarding their pet.

Cornell Diagnostic Database www.vet.cornell. edu/consultant/consult.asp. This site is primarily targeted at veterinarians. The site is sponsored by Cornell University. The database allows a search of diseases by symptom or "signs."

Net Vet netvet.wustl.edu/. The site offers an extensive listing of animal sites, pet sites, scientific sites, medical sites, etc. Visit the virtual zoo and look for site listings by animal.

Free Expert Advice www.petcity.com/. The site offers free veterinarian advice from Dr. Michael W. Fox who answers questions regarding pets, including vaccinations and preventive holistic and alternative medicines, proper nutrition and solving behavior problems, benefits of keeping pets, and the thera-peutic value of animal companions. Under "Ask the Pet Expert," veterinarians, animal behaviorists, vet assistants and others are registered and available to answer questions posted on the message board.

Canada Pets www.canadapets.com/. Free advice from the vet. Pet owners can also browse the database of vet advice. This library contains an assortment of medically related questions concerning caring for your pet. Questions have been answered by Dr. Chip Coombs DVM, while questions regarding pocket pets, exotics, and birds have been answered by Rick Axelson DVM.

While these web sites do not take the place of an in-person consultation with a vet, proper care of pets and pet-owner awareness can often prevent unnecessary trips to the vet.

CHAPTER 4

Other Savings for Your Pet

No animal should ever jump on the dining-room furniture unless absolutely certain that he can hold his own in conversation.

—Fran Lebowitz

The responsibility for a pet doesn't stop with providing food, shelter, health care, hugs and treats now and then. For both you and your pet's benefit, well-being and comfort there are other services you may need from time to time. These include pet-sitting and boarding, grooming and flea control, pet loss support groups, animal training and pet insurance, plus some specialized services. Discounts and money saving opportunities are available if you are willing to spend time researching your options. It will be worth your while to learn as much as possible about the services offered in your area.

Pet Insurance

Did you know?

- Pet owners spend about $11 billion a year on pet health care and total expenditures for veterinary medical services rose almost 30% over the past 5 years.

- Veterinary costs are rising at a rate of almost four times the rate of human health care: 8.1% for pets versus 2.8% for humans.

- Veterinary medical procedures are frequently more expensive than their counterpart would be on a person.

- There are over 6,400 medical diseases and problems that occur in pets.

- Nearly 40% of all visits to the veterinarian by dogs and cats are due to sudden illness or emergencies.

- Costs for veterinary procedures as a result of an automobile accident to your pet could cost $1,000, cancer diagnosis and treatment over $2,500 and intestinal tract problems over $1,000.

- The ability of veterinary medicine to ensure longer life for animals means geriatric dogs and cats contract many of the same chronic illness that humans endure such as diabetes and heart trouble.

- The chances of your pet suffering a serious illness or accident during its lifetime are 50/50.

Many pet owners are still unaware of the existence of pet insurance, which is rapidly gaining acceptance as veterinary fees rise. Today's sophisticated medical diagnoses and procedures have made it possible to save animals where euthanasia would have been the only option a few years ago. Having pet insurance in the case of an accident or serious illness can make the economic difference between saving your pet's life or putting him to sleep.

Most people don't realize how much veterinary care can cost until it's too late and they are forced to make immediate medical and economic decisions. Routine vaccinations and exams—even if not paid by a low-cost or discount program—can lead us to believe that animal medical care is affordable. And it usually is. However, when something unexpected happens to your pet, carrying pet insurance lets you focus on what's best and necessary for your pet instead of on how much it costs.

Pet insurance is probably one of the most confusing types of insurance on the market. Unlike auto insurance and regular health insurance, where you can call 5 different companies and get 5 different prices, the coverage will be basically the same from company to company. With pet insurance, the coverage offered from different companies can be as different as night and day. You as a consumer must understand "what is" and "is not" covered. Your decision can not be based on price alone. If, for example, you own a purebred animal that is prone to physical problems because of genetics, you need to find out if "genetic illness" is covered. Like human medical insurance, pet insurance may not cover ordinary, routine medical care such as vaccinations, certain preexisting conditions and illnesses, cosmetic surgery, grooming and normal checkups. Preventable diseases (those for which vaccines are available) are also not covered.

The growing public awareness of how current state-of-the-art veterinary care can improve a pet's quality of life, the rising cost of pet health care and the evolution of the human/animal bond all contribute to the argument that pet insurance is a viable consideration. Having insurance may not only save you money, but will most likely help you in making an important decision if the need ever arises.

Companies That Offer Pet Insurance

Preferred PetHealth Plus www.pethealthplus. com/index.htm (888-424-4644) is an association of pet owners that provides members with comprehensive pet insurance coverage for their dogs and cats, a nationwide lost and found service, as well as a Pet Pharmacy Program that can save up to 50% on the cost of prescription and non-prescription drugs.

In Canada: PetPlan Insurance at www.petplan.com/ forms/index.html and www.petcareinsurance.com/.

Premier Pet Insurance at www.ppins.com (877-PPI-CARE). Offers three health plans: Premier Basic, which covers illness and injury, plus spaying and neutering; Premier Plus, which covers most routine care (including spaying and neutering) and treatment for illness and injury; and Premier Ultimate, which provides comprehensive coverage for health maintenance (including spaying an neutering) and treatment for illness and injury. There is a $100 annual deductible, and after that they begin reimbursing 80% of the covered expenses. There is immediate coverage for wellness and injuries and a 30-day waiting period for illness coverage. An average annual premium is $120 for Premier Basic, $230 for Premier Plus, and $362 For Premier Ultimate. There is a 10% total premium if you have more than one pet on the same plan.

Veterinary Pet Insurance www.petinsurance. com/ (800-USA-PETS or 800-872-7387). Their Gold Plan has a $40 deductible per incident and an annual benefit maximum of $7,500–$9,000, and a per incident benefit maximum of $2,000–$2,500. Some pre-existing conditions may be covered. They cover accidents, poisonings, illnesses, diagnostics, anesthesia, surgery, hospitalization, X-Rays, specialists, emergency, chemotherapy/radiation, prescriptions, cat scans and MRIs. The policy pays up to 80% of the first $180, and 100% in excess of $180, after the deductible. The annual payment for the Gold Plan is between $109 and $157 for dogs or cats between 2 months and 8 years. They have an Advantage Plus Plan, which pays a maximum annual benefit of $12,000–$14,000 and $4,000–$4,500 maximum per incident. The annual cost of this plan is between $191 and $281.

First Heritage Pet Pak insurance www.firstheritage. com/ins/ins-pet.html. This plan is through First Heritage Insurance. The annual premium is $150.00. The program covers veterinary fees up to $1,000 for each illness and each accident, including hospital-ization, specialist referral and medication; dentistry fees up to $1,000 for extractions as a result of injury; and a maximum claimable amount for total benefits of $1,500 a year. Deductible is $40 per occurrence.

PetsHealth Insurance 877-592-7387 (Toll Free) www.peth.com/default.htm.

Although not insurance, there are two web sites with information about savings programs designed to make veterinary care more affordable:

The JC Penney Pet Club at www.jcpenneypetclub. com/visitors/vetfind.asp offers member discounts and coupons for veterinary care. The program includes 2 free pet exams, discounts on pet products, a pet-ID tag, and special rates on pet insurance. Participating vets offer 20% discount off regular fee for a variety of office services and procedures.

PetAssure www.petassure.com, the Pet Care Savings Program. This company states its purpose as enabling every pet owner to obtain quality healthcare for their extended family members, while aiding in the survival of stray and homeless animals through contributions to SPCAs, humane societies, animal shelters and other animal-related charitable organizations. The program is available through employee benefit programs.

Insurance for Horses
Unlike insurance for dogs and cats, insurance for horses is widely available from a number of different

agencies. Horses, in addition to being great family pets for pleasure riding, are also an investment, especially if you or your children develop an interest in showing. The value of prize winning horses can range from $3,000 to $300,000. The following are agencies with web sites that offer insurance coverage for horses that usually includes mortality, major medical, surgery, theft and loss of use.

Markel Equine www.horseinsurance.com/ 800-842-5017

Fry's Equine Insurance Agency www.frysequine insurance.com/ 800-842-9021

Ace Insurance Services www.aceinsuranceservices.com/ 800-887-9869

B.A. Smith Insurance Associates, www.insure horses.com/

LCI Livestock Insurance, www.lcihorse.com/ 800-874-1789

Equisport Agency, Inc. www.equisportagency.com/ 800-432-1215

Best Insurance Brokerage Ltd. www.bestinsure.com/ or 800-564-9119

Equine Insurance Specialists, www.equispec.com/
800-723-9414

Comprehensive links to other horse insurance
companies is at www.equineinfo.com/services/
insurance.htm

The North American Horsemen's Association
also offers insurance as one of their membership
benefits. For information write: North American
Horsemen's Association, Administrative Offices,
Ark International Group, PO Box 223, Paynesville,
MN 56362, 800-328-8894.

Pet Sitting and Boarding: What to Do with Your Pet When You Travel

Up until a few years ago, the only alternative to
leaving your pets when you went out of town was
either to board them in a kennel or entrust their care
and feeding with a neighborhood kid or friend. If
your pet was the sort that didn't respond well to a
kennel environment (not to mention the possibility
of exposure to illnesses from other animals), being
placed in new surroundings or you didn't quite trust
the neighbor's teenager with your precious companion, neither of these alternatives were satisfactory.
Enter the pet sitting industry.

Pet sitting is a rapidly growing service industry that generated $35 million in 1997. It offers much the other two alternatives do not. Professional pet sitters come to your home and provide a number of services during an average 30 or 40 minute visit. These include: walking your dogs, feeding your pets, bringing in the mail, turning lights on and off, watering plants, forwarding mail and spending quality play time with your pets. Some pet sitters will also provide transportation services such as taking your pet to and from the vet, dropping a pet off at the vet or taking him to the groomer. Some will even sleep at your home, making sure your pet has company through the night and in the morning.

Fees for pet sitting services vary. Most day visits last approximately 40 minutes and can cost as little as $10 a visit up to $30 or more, depending on the area and the services. Depending on your pet's needs, you can have daily or twice daily visits. There are several ways you can find a reliable, reputable pet sitter that provides at-home pet care in your area. First, visit pet shops, groomers and veterinary clinics in your neighborhood and pick up pet sitter brochures or ask them who they recommend. Also, check their bulletin boards for flyers and cards. Check the local newspaper for display or classified ads for pet/house sitting services. The Humane Society in your area may have a pet sitters registry and referral service. There are also organizations that act as information and referral services for member pet sitters.

Pet Sitting Organizations

The National Association of Pet Sitters web site www.petsitters.org offers a locater service and other valuable information for member pet sitters in your area. You can also write them at 1030 15th Street NW, Suite 870, Washington, DC 20006; 202-393-3317.

Pet Sitters Yellow Pages at www.petsitters.com. An extensive listing pet sitter organizations' e-mail and web site links.

Pet Sitters International, www.petsit.com has an online locater service for affiliated pet sitters.

Pet Sitter at www.veternet.com/main-ps.html has a listing of regional pet sitting networks.

Things to consider if you decide to use a pet sitter at www.dogtreat.com/funstuff/petsitters.htm.

Busy Pets at www.busytimes.com/busypets.html has a directory of pet sitters, dog groomers, dog walkers and other pet services.

Pet Net www.pet-net.net has state listings for pet related services such as pet sitters, pet motels, etc.

Atlanta Pet Sitting Service www.atlantapetsitters. com/getknow.htm. This pet-sitting service, based in Atlanta, Georgia, offers a free initial meeting with pets and pet owners to get to know the pet and explain their services.

The Doggie Directory www.doggiedirectory. com/sitters.html has extensive listings for pet sitters, dog boarding services and dog daycare.

HowsMy.com www.howsmy.com offers information on net-cam monitoring of your pet via your computer while you are away.

If it makes you more comfortable, choose a professional pet sitter who is licensed as an Animal Care Consultant, bonded and insured. However, some of the most highly regarded pet care services rely entirely on word of mouth and satisfied client recommendations without regard to certification. Always compare services as well as fees when considering a pet sitter.

A recent alternative to pet sitting is doggie day care. You drop your dog off at a facility for the day (just as you would your child), and pick him up after work, usually by 6:30 P.M. The dog spends the day playing with other dogs—if he's sociable—having snacks, and getting personal attention by a caretaker. It's generally veterinary clinics or hospitals that offer this service, if they have the room to take in animals on a daily basis. The cost is between $25–$35 a day. There are also day camps where you can drop off your pet for the day, or sometimes even overnight.

Kennel Boarding

Animal kennels have come a long way from the days when you would leave to go on vacation and hoped your pet survived the trip. Animal boarding facilities run the gamut from normal to extraordinary services, depending on what you need for your pet and what you are willing to pay. Just as there are all classes of human accommodations from budget motels to fantasy-island luxury resorts, so do kennels range from very modest, but clean and safe, to the ultimate in "home-away-from-homes" for your pet. Rates vary according to amenities and services as they do for human accommodations.

Consider the following services offered by various kennels:

- Three-room suites and condos with attached enclosed patios and/or sunning windows

- 24-hour, on-call veterinary supervision

- Indoor recreation room with television and human companions

- Special diets and medication or healthy, nutritious house diet

- Pet limousine pick-up and relocation service

- Daily playtime and treats

- Temperature controlled environment

- Hotline protection to police and fire stations

- Clean, soft, non-allergic bedding changed daily

- Spa packages, including: pet massage, puppy/kitten care, exercise program, special grooming, geriatric program

- 24-hour residential staff on duty

Does this sound better than your own vacation plans? Seriously, pet boarding kennels (also referred to as Kitty Kastles, Holiday Hotels and Kennel Clubs) want your business and need your recommendations and referrals. However, as always, compare prices for what you need and carefully consider the "extras." Ask your friends for personal recommendations to help you in your search for a trustworthy boarding facility. Most veterinarians offer boarding services at very economical rates. Local pet stores may also offer boarding services.

Tips for owners planning to leave their dog at a kennel: www.canismajor.com/dog/choseken.html.

Kennel listings in California may be found at www.kennelsoft.com/kennels/States/CA.htm.

The American Boarding Kennel Association maintains a web site at www.abka.com/ with listings of member kennels and tips on how to select a boarding kennel. ABKA is a trade association for the pet boarding industry in the U.S. and around the world. AMKA members offer a variety of services including pet boarding, grooming, training, transportation, shipping, pet supplies, day care and food sales. They will also send you free information on their programs and services. Write them at: 1702 East Pikes Peak Avenue, Colorado Springs, CO 80909; 719-667-0116.

Planet Pets.com planetpets.simplenet.com/ boarders.htm offers a boarding directory as well as other information including lists of pet associations online.

Among the information provided by the American Pet Boarding Association are the "Ten Commandments of Pet Boarding" which are excellent guides to follow when choosing a boarding facility. They are:

I. Thou shalt not board in any facility that will not let you see where your pet will be kept.

II. Thou shalt not board in any facility that boards or treats sick animals in the same general area as are kept boarded pets.

III. Thou shall not board in any facility that is not clean and well maintained inside and outside.

IV. Thou shalt not board in any facility that does not require proof of proper vaccinations.

V. Thou shalt not board in any facility that employs immature or incompetent employees to clean and care for the animals.

VI. Thou shalt not board your dog in a cage or pen unless you know it will receive three fifteen minute exercise periods daily, regardless of the weather.

VII. Thou shalt not board your pet in a facility that lacks properly designed ventilation to maintain the ambient temperature between 65° F and 85° F for all warm blooded animals.

VIII. Thou shalt not board your pet in a facility that will not contact your own veterinarian in event of a serious illness or injury.

IX. Thou shalt not board your pet in a facility that does not feed the animals and clean and disinfect their accommodations as required and never less than once in every 24-hour period for warm blooded animals.

X. Thou shalt not board your pet in a facility that permits the boarding of different owners' pets in the same space.

For those owners who can't bear to be separated from their companion animals there are a variety of Internet sites with free information to help them plan a vacation with their pet. When inquiring about whether a hotel or motel accepts pets, be sure to ask if there is a charge. Most accepting establishments do not charge anything additional beyond the room charge, but some will charge up to $75 in addition to what you are paying for the room. Some may also require a deposit which may or may not be refundable.

The Take Your Pet.com at www.takeyourpet.com/pets-motels-01.htm has an online directory for pet friendly lodgings, bulletin boards and other travel resources. Benefits of completing the online membership include a newsletter providing news, tips, and information about traveling with your pet; free Pet

Travel Guides; savings of up to 30% on lodging including discounts at pet-friendly bed and breakfasts, hotels/ motels, inns, and resorts all across the United States, bulletin boards and other resources or the traveler.

PetVacations www.petvacations.com maintains an excellent web site for those contemplating traveling with a pet. It has a search engine that will find pet friendly hotels and motels by state. Post travel tops on the free bulletin board or read tips posted by other pet owners traveling with their pets.

The Animal Protection Institute www.api4animals. org/PetTravel.htm has helpful information for those planning to travel with a companion animal.

Pet-Friendly Hotels www.oregoncitylink.com/ bastian/. Sebastian the Dachsund rates the "pet-friendliness" of hotels in the Pacific Northwest. There is a also a link to a database on pet-friendly hotels around the U.S. If you see a "make reservation" symbol after a listing, you can click on it to make an instant online reservation for that specific lodging.

The Pets Allowed web site at www.jcn1.com/ mbamford/pets_allowed/index.htm has state listings for resorts, lodging, cottages and other lodgings where pets are welcome plus links to books on traveling with a pet

Pet-Friendly Travel Spots www.petswelcome.com/. The travel listings page contains over 25,000 hotels, B&Bs, ski resorts, campgrounds, and beaches that are pet-friendly. The "Travel Info" section helps pet owners learn how to take their pet anywhere. Or visit the "Info Xchange" to find answers from millions of other sophisticated travelers.

The I-95 Travel Bookstore web site www.usastar. com/books/pets.htm features a number of books on traveling with pets.

Helpful Literature

- The Tours books from the American Automobile Association

- *Traveling with Towser* ($3.00) from Quaker Professional Services, TWT, Dept. CCC, 585 Hawthorne Court, Galesburg, IL 61401

- *The Pets Allowed Directory* ($12.95 plus $2.00 s/h) from American Media Group, 7300 W. 110th St., Suite 960, Overland Park, KS 66210

- *Traveling With Your Pet* is posted at the ASPCA web site at www.usastar.com/books/pets.htm. There is also an online form for receiving coupons from ASPCA sponsors.

- Frommer's *On the Road Again with Man's Best Friend*, editions by state ($14.95). A Dawbert Press, Inc. publication. McMillan USA.

- *Eileen's Directory of Pet-Friendly Lodging*, United States and Canada.($19.95) Pet-Friendly Publications, PO box 8459, Scottsdale, AZ 85252, 800-496-2665.

Pet Galaxy Web site at www.animall.com/pets_travelinks.html maintains a list of travel links.

The Air Transport Association of America has information on traveling with pets. Visit their site at: www.air-transport.org/public/public/pets/Default.htm. They also have free publications.

Betty White's web site, Travelingdog has links for online pet travel guide and listings of pet-friendly accommodations. Go to www.travelingdogs.com/dogvacations.html.

The Pet Safety Center web site www.familysafety.com/travel/auto/car.shtml has valuable information about traveling with a pet, as well as a pet lodging link.

Of vital importance when traveling with a pet is knowing what to do if it gets lost. The Pet Club of America www.petclub.org/benefits.htm, 800-666-

5678, has a travel protection and lost pet finding service. Their benefits include: a pet tag with a serial number and 24-hour phone number; a database of thousands of found pets; Lost Pet Report fax service to facilities that take in strays over a 60 mile radius of where the pet was lost; guarantee of payment to a veterinarian if your pet has been injured; personalized travel assistance that includes current lists of hotels that accept pets; emergency door and window decals that alert police and fire departments of the number and types of pets that need rescue in an emergency; publications which offer suggestions for trouble-free travel with pets. Pet registration costs $15. Register all of your pets online and save $5 on each additional pet, a 33% savings over the regular annual registration fee!

Sending Your Pet to School

All dogs, cats and many birds require training of some kind in order to live harmoniously with their human families. (Horses and other ranch and farm animals need extensive training as well, but we've limited our discussion to pets in the home.) The desire for a pleasurable, faithful, trustworthy companion and pet is the primary reason most people choose to have an animal in their home. Cute little kittens and puppies only stay "cute" for a short time. Sooner than you think, they've grown into full size animals who believe, since your home is their home, they can behave in any wild, unruly and destructive way they please. Dogs, especially, can be trained beginning as early as seven weeks of age, thus preventing most adult behavior and obedience problems.

Training cats and birds is usually related to specific problems, habits or behaviors that are unacceptable. Some are taught particular tricks or specialty stunts. In the case of birds, many owners hire professional trainers to teach them to talk. There are also many books and videos on the subjects of taming and training particular species to talk and do tricks. Check with pet shops that specialize in birds for recommendations of personal trainers. They can aid you in taming your pet as well advice on breeding, choosing a bird, health, nutrition, housing and grooming.

Since the majority of pet training services are for dogs, we are going to focus on the methods and choices available. There are a wide variety of philosophies regarding dog training that can range in cost accordingly. Basically, you can train your pet in one of three ways:

- In-home training. The trainer comes to your home for a series of sessions and trains you and your pet(s) in the familiar surroundings of your family and home.

- Away-from-home training with owner. You and your pet go to a facility (training school, playground, community center or park) and receive your training together in a series of classes.

- Away-from-home training without owner. You send your pet to be trained at a boarding "dog school" for a specific length of time.

Or, in addition to the above, you can use:
- Telephone training. A few highly trained animal behaviorists and psychotherapists will counsel pet owners about behavioral problems over the phone.

Training programs are also developed for dogs according to their age and whether they have specific problems that need to be eliminated. These are generally broken down into: Puppy training (from 7–16 weeks); Basic adult obedience training (16 weeks and up); and problem-solving training (i.e. jumping on people, chewing, aggression, running away or into the street, excessive barking, etc.). Obedience training can include both on-leash or more advanced off-leash training, in addition to teaching basic commands. There are also specialized training programs for theatrical and stunt work, protection, guide dogs and hunting dogs.

Often when a pet's environment changes drastically, as when moving to a new home, the arrival of a new baby or the departure of a principal companion, they need to be acclimated to these stressful changes. There is special training for these situations as well. In-home training programs are individualized, one to two hour sessions where the trainer comes to your home, often working with different members of your family to train your pet. The comfortable, familiar surroundings are conducive to training as the pet may be more relaxed and able to concentrate on his lessons. Also, specific problems that occur at home can be dealt with in the same surroundings in which they occur.

Most courses run from five to ten weeks and cost between $300 and $1500 for a complete once-a-week program. Some trainers also offer individual sessions for problems that may not require a whole series. In these cases they charge a set hourly or per-session rate. Most trainers offer a free consultation to evaluate your pet. When choosing an "in-home" program, make sure the trainer guarantees his work and will retrain you and your dog free of charge at any time if backsliding occurs.

The most familiar (and least expensive) example of away-from-home training with an owner are puppy and dog training classes offered by city and county Parks and Recreation Departments. They are usually taught by private professional trainers who offer these low-cost classes to the public. The classes take place at school playgrounds, parks, community centers or other public places. Classes usually meet once a week in the evening, making it convenient for those who work during the day. One positive element of this type of training is that your dog becomes socialized and learns to behave around other animals in a class with ten or more other dogs. However, if your dog is easily distracted, having this many new friends around may keep you and him from concentrating on the lesson at hand. Prices for six to eight week classes range from $40 to $85 and many offer discounts to senior citizens. Some private instructors also offer classes at their schools in addition to one-on-one instruction. These usually cost under $100. Check local newspapers and community calendar segments on radio and television to find out when these "good dog" classes are held in your area.

You can also board your dog in a school kennel where he is taught the techniques of obedience, house training and proper behavior. This is individualized, private training where, after two to six weeks, you pick up your trained dog. There is usually at least one session with the owner to familiarize him with what his dog has learned while at boarding school. Costs for this type of training are similar to at-home training, plus the added expenses of food and board.

Contact the National Association of Dog Obedience Instructors www.nadoi.org/ for a listing of approved member trainers. You can also write them at : NADOI,

Attn: Corresponding Secretary, PMB #369, 729 Grapevine Hwy, Suite 369, Hurst, TX 76054-2085.

Animal Training Videos

If you have chosen to tackle the job of training your pet yourself, your first thought might be to find books on the various training techniques. You can easily find dozens of helpful sources detailing all phases of training of animals. Many are available free from the shelves of your local library.

However, as the saying goes, a picture is worth a thousand words. That's where animal training videos are really worth the price. The most effective way for you to attain success in do-it-yourself training is by seeing exactly what you should be doing and what your animal should be doing in response to your commands. Also, by training at home, you can go at your own pace, spending as little or as much time as you and your pet require. Most training videos cost between $17.95 and $49.95. Specialty videos, such as protection training, may cost more. Many contain useful information on nutrition, healthcare, grooming, etc.

Ask your veterinarian or local pet store for recommendations on training videos. Many are advertised in pet magazines and offer free information and catalogs. Animal supply catalogs also offer books and videos. Specialty bookstores usually carry videotapes and audio cassettes in addition to books.

Free Internet information about dog training and obedience and directories for professional dog trainers:

The LearnFree.com web site at <u>www.training yourdog.com</u> has a free online dog training VidBook that teaches basic dog obedience exercises.

Free Pet Software and CDs <u>www.chazhound.com/</u>. Chazhound offers free software on pet management. The site also has many useful articles and resources that can be used offline or online right from your computer. This includes the free Puppy and Adult Training Course. Download a free dog screensaver featuring Nimby's "Not in My Backyard" cartoon scripts. PetServ also offers a free pet management Web-CD. You'll have all the resources a pet owner needs, from care tips, vet tracker and vaccination charts, to expert advice and your own Pet Site.

Sign up for daily e-mail dog training tips at <u>affiliate. freeshop.com/pg02581.htm</u>.

The American Dog Trainers Network web site <u>www.inch.com/~dogs/index.htm</u> has a directory, online articles and other links to free information.

Learn dog training tips at <u>www.apolitepooch.com/</u>. This site is edited by Dog Trainers, who offer free advice under "Poochie Pointers" www.apolitepooch. com/pointers.asp.

The ASPCA maintains a search engine for the American Pet Dog Trainers at www.apdt.com/trainer.htm.

Best Paw Forward www.bestpaw.com/bpftrain. html has links to dog training information.

Canines of America www.canines.com/coanetwork has trainer's directory.

Pooch and Meow www.poochandmeow.com. This site offers a free tutorial on pet training. Pet owners can have a free phone consultation with an expert animalogist who will answer their pet training questions

Dr. P's Dog Training www.uwsp.edu/acad/psych/ dog/dog.htm is a comprehensive online site for information. The site's library link www.uwsp.edu/ acad/psych/dog/lib-SpecTrain.htm has an extensive list of online articles covering all aspects of dog training, obedience and behavior.

Dogpatch web site www.dogpatch.org/obed/ obpage2.cfm has links to basic training information.

Final Solution Dog Training www.dog-training.com/trainers.htm#top has a list of schools across the country.

Houssen's Dog Training Center www.houssen.com has free introductory materials on its web site for downloading.

John's Natural Dog Training Company www.johnknowsdogs.com/dearjohn.htm offers an online form for questions on dog training and behavior.

Pet Place at www.ddc.com/petplace/dogtraining has a series of articles on dog training.

The Doggie Door www.doggiedoor.com has dog training and behavior information, including message boards covering various topics for questions and answers.

The Leerburg Video and Kennel web site www.leerburg.com has information on dog training videos.

VideoLine www.video-line.com/dog.html offers a dog training video.

Whichever training method you choose, we recommend reading *Mother Knows Best: The Natural Way to Train Your Dog*, by Carol Benjamin. It is an excellent guide that will supplement any training program. It can be ordered online at the Pet Expo web site, www.pet-expo.com/trainbooks.htm#train which also has numerous other dog training books and videos.

Animal Behaviorists

Sometimes a problem with a dog goes beyond learning proper behavior. In that case, there are a growing number of animal behaviorists who offer counseling by telephone. They usually have a strong background in animal or human psychology and can determine the causes of problems and how to deal with them by the owner's descriptions of the animal's behavior. Whatever problem you are experiencing with your pet, it may be solvable through a long distance specialist.

Since many animals end up in shelters because of behavior problems, many shelters such as the ASPCA www.aspca.org offer behavioral therapy in addition to dog training.

The Animal Behavior Center of New York offers information on telephone consultations at its web site canines.com/abcny/consult.shtml.

Dr. C. Meisterfeld, a canine psychoanalyst, whose web site can be found at www.dogwhisper.com/services.html offers telephone consultations and books.

Savings on Pet Grooming

Nothing is worse than a dirty dog, except perhaps a dirty dog with fleas. Cats, by nature, are self-cleaning animals, but even cats get fleas, ticks or occasionally end up in a mud puddle or get caught in a downpour. Professional grooming services can include a haircut, flea bath and dip, medicated bath, nail clipping, ear cleaning, teeth cleaning and skin and coat conditioning.

The least expensive way to groom your dog is to do it yourself at home. You can buy professional pet grooming products, such as clippers, trimmers, nail cutters, etc. at a discount through most pet supply catalogs. However, if your dog requires a special haircut or shave, you might want to send him to the groomer between baths. If your dog has an especially bad case of fleas, we suggest you invest in a professional flea bath and dip during those times when infestation is at its worst.

Most veterinarians offer bathing and nail clipping and many also have staff that can do basic grooming to maintain your dog or cat's coat. If your dog's breed requires a specialized haircut you may have to go to a full-service groomer and drop your dog off for the day. Recently, mobile groomers, where the groomer comes to your home and provides services from a fully equipped pet salon on wheels, have developed. In fact, the range of mobile pet services now include the convenience of having a vet come to your home; getting food delivered to your door; having a professional trainer come to you; pet-sitting and taxi services to deliver your pet in style; personalized counseling for your pet; and door-to-door flea elimination service.

Professional grooming services range from around $18 for small, short haired dogs to $35 or more for large, long haired dogs. For cats, prices range between $17 and $25. Full service grooming—which includes a shampoo, nail trimming, ear cleaning, flea bath and dip or medicated bath—can cost between $35 to $75 depending on the size of the dog.

When checking on prices, ask if there are any discounts or specials being offered. Some groomers will offer from 10 to 20 percent off a full-service grooming or select extra services. Some grooming salons offer special rates and services to individuals with assistance dogs.

Internet Sites on Grooming

Costalpet at www.coastalpet.com/products/dgtips.htm has grooming tips and information for owners.

Petgroomer.com at www.petgroomer.com/petowner.htm is an excellent web site for information on the pet grooming industry. There is also a variety of resources for all pet enthusiasts, including free newsgroups for dog and cat owners and support for those who have lost a pet. This page www.petgroomer.

com/index3.html has a directory of professional groomers.

National Dog Groomers Association of America, www.nauticom.net/www/ndga/; 412-962-2711.

The NY School of Dog Grooming has a free booklet on learning dog grooming by calling 1-800-541-5541.

What If Your Pet Gets Lost or Stolen?

Just as you should consider health insurance for your pet, you might want to consider one the following, low cost "insurance" services. Unlike collars, these methods for protecting your pet cannot be removed-a major benefit if your pet is likely to get lost or stolen. Any vet who treats the animal later may spot a tattoo or scan for a microchip. So might employees of research facilities where many stolen animals end up.

The American Pet Association www.apapets.com/ Members.htm has several pet recovery programs for the price of $12.95 (through the web) membership.

Companion Pet Care Network at www.idpet.com has a free pet registry and free pet ID offer.

Missing Pet Network www.missingpet.net/ anlost.html. This registry is a database of lost or found pets. Submit or search for a pet by state or by country. The database includes a dedicated registry for lost or stolen horses.

Purina O.N.E. web site www.purinaone.com/homeFrameSet.asp has a free dog safety kit with a sticker for emergency personnel

Drs. Foster & Smith web site drsfostersmith.com offers a free engraved dog name tag.

Pet tattoo information is at www.btwf.org/tattoo.htm.

Tattoo-A-Pet www.tattoo-a-pet.com/information.html (800-828-8667; info@tattoo-a-pet.com) offers pet owners the opportunity to have their dog painlessly tattooed with an identification number that is nationally registered. There are over 3,000 veterinarians affiliated with this association and the fee is $35 for the first pet and $10 for the second. Each pet is then given a special tag with the toll-free lost and found hotline telephone number. They also run a nonprofit tattoo operation in many shelters across the country. Once an animal is adopted, the adoption agency tattoos the pet. This permanent identification of your pet helps prevent theft and provides a much greater chance of recovery if it is lost.

National Dog Registry www.natldogregistry.com; 800-637-3647. Founded in 1966, the National Dog Registry is the largest animal recovery agency in the world. By tattooing an identification number on the right hind leg of your pet and then nationally registering the animal with this organization, you can help prevent the theft of your animal and greatly enhance its chance of recovery. The group maintains a 24-hour hotline every day of the year, and with over three million animals now registered, they have a recovery rate of over 95 percent. They work with smaller pet identification agencies, such at Tattoo-A-Pet, to help locate animals and their owners. They offer a network of over 5,000 animal welfare officials who engrave the tattoo identification number, usually for just $10. There is a one-time fee of $35 for a member to join the registry. This fee covers the registration of all the animals you have or will have during your lifetime.

There are several other organizations and registries that operate identification registries or services. These organizations may be able to assist you in determining the identity and ownership of a lost or abandoned dog that bears a tattoo, specific registry ID tag, or evidence of microchip.

The Pet Galaxy Registration web site at www.petgalaxy.com/f_health_reg_id.html has a list of regional organizations with whom owners can register their pets.

AKC Companion Animal Recovery www.akc.org/Car.htm, 800-252-7894, Fax: 919-233-1290, E-mail: found@akc.org.

National Pet Registry www.americanpetregistry.com/. Through this service, your pet is assigned an identification number unique to them. All of the information is then kept in a secure database accessible only by the staff at The American Pet Registry. An identification medallion and a wallet card will be sent to the pet owner. The medallion will be engraved with the pet's name, the identification number, and a toll free telephone number. The wallet card will have the same information, but will include the owner's name and the pet's picture for identification purposes when recovering them from a facility.

Identipet-Tel: 800-243-9147. They are a tatoo registry.

National Animal ID Center (Natchez, MS) 800-647-6761

National Stock Dog Registry (Butler, IN) 800-538-7677

Pet Protection Plus (Memphis, TN) 800-238-7387

US Kennel Club, Inc. (Bellmore, NY) 800-352-8752

Pet Club of America www.petclub.org, 800-666-5678, operates Petfinders, a non-profit pet finding agency.

Petfinder.org www.petfinder.org/search.html offers a pet search engine.

AWOLPET.com at www.awolpet.com/ is the first web-based pet registration system that allows you to register your pet using its rabies tag, license tag, micro chip and/or tattoo codes. Any and all of your pet's identifiers can be registered to make sure that whoever finds your pet can quickly and easily find you. You can also register your pet's daily medication needs. Once registered, you will receive a small red square tag for your pet to wear with its current tag. This alerts the finder to visit www.awolpet.com to find your pet's home. Initial registration of a pet costs $7, but use of the database is free to anyone. Volume discounts are given for registration of more than one pet, so that the fourth pet is free.

American Veterinary Identification Devices www.avidid.com. Registration and Recovery Services (PETtrac) 800-336-AVID.

HomeAgain IdentIchip www.identichip.com. Identification Recovery System Registration and Recovery Services, 800-926-1313.

InfoPET Systems Registration and Recovery Services: 800-INFOPET.

PetNet-Canada: 1-800-PETNETS.

Lost My Pet.com www.lostmypet.com has an online form and ID tag ($11.45) for Internet pet registry good for two years.

Pet Guardian Angels of America www.pgaa.com/justfaq.html#what has a pet ID tag and registry.

When a Pet Dies—Pet Support Groups

Losing a special animal can be a very difficult, sensitive time. Although friends and family may be supportive, they may not be able to offer the care and understanding that is needed to get through this period of loss. Children and the elderly, especially, who often depend on pets as a primary source of companionship, may need special counseling. There are pet loss support groups, hotlines and seminars especially created for people who have experienced the death of a pet. Many of them are free and meet at veterinary offices or community centers. Check announcements in your local papers for times and locations.

Internet sites with helpful information for people who have lost a pet:

The official Web site of the ASPCA www.aspca.org/ offers a wide variety of resources, including pet adoption, and free counseling on the loss of a pet. Stephanie LaFarge, Ph.D., The ASPCA's Director of Counseling Services, is available—at no charge—to talk with anyone who is coping with loss or other relationship issues. She can help with: deciding on euthanasia; attending to the special needs of children, older adults and differently-abled individuals; making arrangement for the animal's remains; helping surviving pets relate to the loss of their companion and deciding when to bring home a new companion.

The American Animal Hospital Association www. healthypet.com/Library/bond-10.html has articles on dealing with a pet's death and and a listing of pet support hotlines.

The American Veterinary Medical Association at www.avma.org/care4pets/losshotl.htm has a list of grief support hotlines.

Accredited counseling centers and hotlines at www.aplb.org/hotline.htm#C.

Animal News.com at www.animalnews.com/ memorial/resources.htm has a directory of pet loss support groups.

American Dog Trainers Network www.inch.com/~dogs/grief.html posts a list of grief counselors.

Do dogs go to heaven? Find out at the Dog Heaven web site at www.dogheaven.com.

The Pet Loss Books web site www.petloss.com/amazon/booklist.htm has listings of books that can help pet owners cope with the death of their pet.

The College of Veterinary Medicine at the Unviersity of Illinois net.cvm.uiuc.edu/CARE maintains a grief hotline for people who have lost their pets and also offers e-mail at griefhelp@cvm.uiuc.edu.

Do pets have souls? See www.arktrust.org/animals/books/petsouls.htm before making up your mind.

A registry of pet bereavement counselors is at aplb.org/counsel.htm.

The Association for Pet Loss and Bereavement maintains web site at www.aplb.org for grieving pet owners.

Iowa State University www.vm.iastate.edu/support/weblink.html has a Pet Loss Support Hotline 1-888-ISU-PLSH.

Forever Pets www.foreverpets.com/B-PetLoss Support.html has pet loss support resources, links and a hotline.

Cornell University Pet Hotline web.vet.cornell. edu/public/petloss/sites.htm has a small collection of other sites that are relevant to the subject of pet loss, each with a brief description.

Kathleen Dunn, a pet loss grief counselor at the University of Pennsylvania School of Veterinary Medicine can be reached at kldunn@vet.upenn.edu.

Virtual Pet Cemetery www.mycemetery.com/my/ pet_menu.html. Submit a pet's epitaph to have it placed in the free online cemetery. The cemetery is searchable by plot number and location.

Online Pet Loss Support Ceremony www.petloss. com/. This site is offered as a support group for people who are mourning the loss of a pet. On Monday evenings all across the globe participants light candles in memory of lost pets. The site states, "It is a very healing ritual with no adherence to any religion or creed, just a simple lighting of candles to bring us all together. The Candle Ceremony is not done online. Each of us lights our candles in our own way."

Pet Chat at www.kathiethaw.com is devoted to helping people who are in grief over the loss of a beloved pet. On this site you can find resources which will hopefully help those in bereavement over the loss of a dear pet.

The Delta Society www.petsforum.com/deltasociety/dsn300.htm offers pet loss and bereavement support hotlines/telephone support.

There are also several excellent books on the subject of loss including:

Loving and Losing a Pet: A Psychologist and a Veterinarian Share Their Wisdom, Michael Stern.

It's Okay to Cry, Maria L. King.

Angel Pawprints: Reflections on Loving and Losing a Canine Companion, Laurel E. Hunt.

Journey Through Pet Loss, Deborah Antinori, Audio Cassette.

Pet Loss: A Thoughtful Guide for Adults and Children, Nieburg and Fischer, Harper & Row.

When Your Pet Dies: How to Cope with Your Feelings, Quackenbush and Graveline, Simon and Schuster.

Coping with Sorrow & Loss Of Your Pet, Anderson, Peregrine Press.

How to Survive the Loss of A Love, Bloomfield, Bantam Books

Helping Children to Cope with Separation and Loss, Jewett, Harvard Common.

Lifetimes, Mellonie and Ingpen, Bantam Books.

The Tenth Good Thing About Barney, Viorst, Atheneum.

When Bad Things Happen To Good People, Kushner, Avon.

Special Services for Fido and Fluffy

Aside from the "normal" pet services already covered, special discounts on unusual services include:

• *Pet acupuncture*
This treatment helps pets in the same way it helps humans, especially those with arthritis and joint problems. Relief for organic problems has also been successful. Non-invasive treatment administered at acupuncture points on the animal's body has proven effective and long-term in many cases. The Alternative Veterinary Medicine web site www.altvetmed.com/index1.html and www.bnatural.com/animals/holvet.

htm have links and information and directories on alternative pet therapies such as acupuncture.

• *Animal communicators*

Animal communicators have the ability to receive and send mental images to animals to solve emotional, behavioral and physical problems. According to one pet communicator, "Our pets have thoughts and emotions just as we do. Understanding your animal's feelings offers a chance to discover the unique role you play in each other's lives. Whether it is simply to have a fun and exciting time getting to know your pet better or to solve a behavior problem, telepathic communication can help open a new awareness between you and your pet."

At www. petinsight.com you can learn all about this fascinating world from pet communicator, Sharen Martinson. Sharen will communicate with your pet by e-mail, mail or telephone (818-880-4216). Your animal need not be present. Carol Gurney of Thousand Oaks, California is an animal communicator who, through her workshops (she also offers telephone consultation), teaches owners of all types of pets, from dogs to horses, to understand the language of their animals. Maureen Hall of Sylmar, California has over 30 years experience as an animal trainer, communicator and behavior consultant.

Links to a variety of animal communicator web sites can be found at: www.holistichorse.com/

directory/communication.html and animaltalk.net/animal%20communicators.htm

Other animal communicator sites include: home.maine.rr.com/headtoheart and www.awarenessmag.com/nd_brigi.htm

There is an online animal communicator newsletter at www.anitacurtis.com/newsletter.htm

Pet Psychic globalpsychics.com/lp/Animalstalk/summer.htm. Pet psychic gives free advice on communicating freely with pets. Submit specific questions to the psychic globalpsychics.com/lp/Animalstalk/tips.htm and the answer may be posted on the bulletin board.

- *Discounts on training for adopted, rescued or neutered pets.*
As supporters of the movement in pet population control, some trainers give a discount if you acquired your pet through a rescue or adoption service and have had him neutered. Ask local trainers if they offer such a discount.

- *Free puppy selection service.*
If you feel you need help in selecting your new dog or puppy before you take him home, ask a trainer if he/she will help you choose your new

housemate. Professional trainers are very sensitive to the disposition of animals and can guide you in picking a pet or breed that best meets your home situation and needs. Of course, they may want you to use them when you begin your pet's training program.

• *Home delivery of pet food and pet supplies.*

Some manufacturers will deliver their pet food. If you know the brand of pet food you prefer, call the toll-free number of the manufacturer and ask whether they deliver in your area. Your vet or local pet store may also know about high quality pet food delivery services.

For example, Consolidated Pet Foods in Southern California will deliver an assortment of foods to the Los Angeles and Orange County areas. They have been in business for over 25 years. They offer dry food, all natural frozen meat loaf, canned foods and holistic pet food. They deliver to your home every two weeks. They charge $1.85 for delivery plus the cost of the food. Home delivery may cost a little more, but in many cases, especially for housebound, ill or elderly per owners, the service they provide greatly outweighs the small delivery charge.

Many pet stores also offer free delivery service, not just on large bulky items (40 lb. Bags of food or aquariums), but also fish. These services are normally available by request from premium pet centers.

• *Pet transportation services.*

In addition to delivering pet food and supplies, there are also pet "limousine" services that provide emergency transportation, discounts on pet transportation and other benefits. These services are generally provided by boarding kennels and veterinary hospitals from which pets have to be transported when their owners are not available. However, there are also private pet taxi services that provide transportation. The Kennel Club of So. California www. kennelclublax.com advertises worldwide transport, limo service, health documentation, shipping kennels and luxury boarding.

• *Free veterinary exams.*

Most veterinarians vehemently support the pet population control movement. Some offer free health evaluations and exams for dogs and cats that have been rescued or adopted from a shelter. Ask your vet if he provides this service.

CHAPTER 5

Everything You've Always Wanted to Know About Your Pet: Free Magazines, Newsletters, Books and More

The great pleasure of a dog is that you may make a fool of yourself with him and not only will he not scold you, but he will make a fool of himself, too.

—Samuel Butler

With very little effort and cost (in fact, usually for free), you can find out everything you need to know about living with and caring for your pets. Informative, educational, entertaining booklets and brochures covering every aspect of pet care are readily available for free at your local vet's office, pet supply store, kennel club, grooming shop or by sending away for a copy. Much of the information is provided by pet food manufacturers who hope that once you've read their helpful tips and hints, you will buy their products. Whether you decide to buy their products is up to you; however, you can't beat the price for the amount of knowledge you get in return-it's all for free!

It used to be that the best free source for access to information in books and magazines was the public library. Even libraries in small rural communities have books on pet care, training, and animal health and many have subscriptions to popular pet-related magazines and also have back issues on file. Liberal renewal policies and some note taking skills are all you need to get information and have it handy for future reference.

However, with the advent of the Internet and the World Wide Web, online users have instant access to information sources that were never before accessible on a local level. As you will see s click will nearly always get you the free information you need about caring for your pet(s).

Free Online Information from Pet Food Companies
• *Ralston Purina Company*
Located at www.ralston.com, the Ralston Purina Company offers pet owners the chance to ask them

questions about your pet. Just click on the "How can we help?" link to get advice. Furthermore, you can learn to keep your pet safe by ordering the free Pet Safety Kit at www.purinaone.com/homeFrameSet. asp. This kit is filled with information on pet rescue, pet emergency care and pet health. Read the booklet to learn about specific health threats for cats and dogs.

Also from Ralston Purina Company, learn everything you need to know about dogs and cats at www.purina.com/dogs/index.html and www. purina.com/cats/index.html. The site offers a vast amount of information about nutrition, training and behavior, health and grooming, and features the *Purina Encyclopedia of Dog/Cat Care*. This is a great site for brand new pet owners.

- *Hill's Prescription Diet*

This web site www.hillspet.com/ offers a huge amount of nutrition and health facts about your cat and dog. Going to their health center can provide all the needed information about pet ailments. Information can be found about liver disease, kidney disease, heart disease and further disorders. They offer pet owners access to nutritional facts as well as information about how to pick a veterinarian. For preventive care, Hill provides recovery tips to speed up the healing process. At the same time, learn to properly care for your pet online at no cost. For pet owner needs, simply search for what you would like to learn about, for example digestive diseases, using the Hill's Site Search.

- For specific articles about heart disease go to: www.hillspet.com/vets/clinical/articles/heart%5Fdisease.html or www.hillspet.com/public/health_center/disease/heart_disease.html

- For specific articles on Feline Urologic Syndrome go to: www.hillspet.com/vets/clinical/atlas/71.html

- For a very informative site containing articles about pet ailments go to: www.hillspet.com/vets/clinical/index.html

- For information about older dogs go to: www.hillspet.com/stage/health_center/dogs/older/index.html

- From Science Diet (also from Hill's Science Diet): The ideal site to find pet foods and treats that are formulated to help keep dogs and cats healthy www.sciencediet.com/public/products/sd/index.asp

- *Friskies*

A nice fact about pet products is that Nestlé acquired Carnation in 1985 and recently, the brand Alpo. At Friskies.com, you will find information on dog and cat behavior, provided information about nutrition and proper pet care, vet information, as well as a pet care resource with a vast amount of information. Simply go online to www.friskies.com/frisky_pet. asp.

• *Alpo*
Learn to teach your dog to play Frisbee in this site: www.friskypet.com/al/al_hp_intro.html

Learn the Latest from Newsletters

Most organizations centered around the care and keeping of a particular pet or animal provide information to their members and other interested individuals. Horse organizations and breed clubs for dogs (i.e. Recycled Rotts www.recycledrotts.org/archive/rrnews1a.html), cats and birds, ferrets, rats and mice and guinea pigs, to name a few, publish their own newsletter or magazine. Likewise most organizations and associations that are involved in animal rights and similar causes such as humane societies and SPCAs publish informative monthly or quarterly newsletters. These newsletters are either "online" or else are sent to an e-mail address. The elimination of postage and printing means many of these are free.

Online "E-Zines"

The advent of the Internet and the World Wide Web has opened a whole new arena in the area of information availability in the form of "e-zines," which are web pages designed like a magazine with articles and photographs. These can be viewed on line and the individual can send the pages to his or her own printer to obtain a hard copy for future reference. Sometimes e-zines are in the form of PDF files which must be read by Adobe Acrobat Reader which (available free at www.adobe.com). Some e-zines are Internet versions of print magazines, others are web pages sponsored by breed clubs, organizations or individuals who are experts in a particular field of pet care. With rare exception, the online "e-zines" are free and so are most of the e-mail newsletters.

An extensive list of pet-related magazines is at www.petgalaxy.com/f_library_zines.html.

Most breed clubs for dogs, cats and birds publish their own newsletter or magazine, Write to the club or organization and ask for a sample issue and subscription information. If you are interested in a specific breed of dog, cat or bird you can contact the following registries and associations for addresses of national and local breed clubs and societies. More complete lists can be found at www.planetpets.simplenet.com/petassoc.htm or www.petstoz.com:

- American Kennel Club www.akc.org, 5580 Centerview Drive, Raleigh, NC 27606.

- United Kennel Club www.ukcdogs.com, 100 E. Kilgore Rd., Kalamazoo, MI 49001, 616-343-9020.

- Federation of International Canines www.ficregistry.org/mainpage.htm, FIC, PO Box 250307 Montgomery, AL, 36125-0307.

- National Kennel Clubs lists can be found at: www.crosswinds.net/~skyefearie/nkc.html.

- The Cat Fanciers' Association, Inc. www.cfainc.org, PO Box 1005, Manasquan, NJ 08736-0805. 732-528-9797.

- The International Cat Association www.tica.org/regularpage.htm.

- The American Cat Fancier's Association www.acfacat.com, PO Box 203, Point Lookout, MO 65726. 417-334-5430, E-mail: info@acfacat.co.

- Other Cat Club links at: www.petplanet.nl/cats/links/clubs.html.

- American Federation of Aviculture (AFA) www.blackstone-aviaries.com/afa.html. PO Box 56218, Phoenix, AZ 85079. 602-484-0931.

- International Aviculturists Society (IAS) www. funnyfarmexotics.com/IAS, PO Box 2232 LaBelle, FL 33975.

Links to other bird clubs and organizations are at www.animall.com/pets_birdlinks.html and www. auburnweb.com/foothill_bird/links.html.

Acme Pet.com acmepet.petsmart.com/club/ bboard/index.html has free message boards and chat rooms covering pets of all types, including dogs, cats, horses, birds, and small animals.

AllPets.com www.allpets.com/flash/mainflash.htm has an online magazine, free e-mail updates on special offers and a personal networking service for animal lovers. This is the perfect place to meet people who love their pets as much as you do, whether you are looking for a friendship, a companion or a serious relationship, at www.SinglePetPeople.com you have something in common right from the start-a love for pets!

At www.petsatoz.com you will find a comprehensive directory of pet links and information. Categories include:
- Canine/Dog Clubs and Associations

- Dog Kennel Clubs

- Feline/Cat Clubs & Associations

- Online Pet Magazines

- Pet health Links

- Pet Food Brands

- Stores & Catalogs

- *Pet Magazine* Subscriptions (includes free trial offers)

Dr. Lowell Ackerman, a well-known veterinarian, has authored a number of articles at the web site www.parentzone.com/petzone/health/dog/index.html which has extensive online information about pet care.

Animal Essentials www.animalessentials.com/newsletter/newsletter2.cfm has a free online newsletter on animal health.

Avian Publications www.avianpublications.com/wob.htm offers Words on Birds, an e-mail newsletter.

Bargain Dog www.bargaindog.com/?adid=T5040 offers a free e-mail newsletter updated with sales and online shopping bargains.

Birds—An online book on caring for pet birds is located at: www.ddc.com/~kjohnson/birdcare.htm.

Birds e-zines are also at:
—www.voren.com and
—www.birdsnways.com/wisdom/ww31e.htm

Buckeye Pet Foods buckeyenutrition.com/pet/index.html offers an e-mail newsletter "Paws for Thoughts" and an online form to request information and coupons.

Canine Book Store at www.puppydogweb.com/bookstore/bookstore.htm has a free newsletter.

Cats Aimee Pet Care Tips at www.pws.vi/Cats/Aimee/Pet_Care_Tips/pet_care_tops.html has tips on what signs to watch out for if your pet has an ailment and whether you should go to your vet.

Catzbuzz members.aol.com/catsbuzz/free.htm has a free book offer for ordering online.

Cavies Galore www.caviesgalore.com has free forums and e-mail updates, online games and general information on guinea pigs.

Chazhound www.chazhound.com/petgames.html has a free dog e-book.

Chickens—A newsletter for owners of pet ornamental bantam chickens is at www.wcinet.net/~quakes/.

The Cornell Feline Health Center, College of Veterinary Medicine at Cornell University web site www.vet.cornell.edu/Public/FHC/brochure.html has online brochures reporting on a variety of cat-related issues.

Dr. Dan www.dr-dan.com/newslett.htm has a free e-mail *Pet Stuff* newsletter.

Drs. Foster & Smith drsfostersmith.com has free e-mail newsletters for dog and pet owners. This site, run by veterinarians, offers pet products, services and advice, including a ". . . including hundreds of informative articles on pet healthcare, written by veterinary experts. Our site has many other features including directories, a veterinary dictionary, answers to frequently asked questions, quizzes, and the latest news. With information on dog and cat behavior, puppy training, nutrition, housebreaking, diseases, parasites, grooming, arthritis and more—you'll find the information and services you need for a healthy, happy pet."

Duff the Hamster web page www.homestead. com/DuffTheHamster has a free e-mail pamphlet on hamster care.

Duncraft www.duncraft.com maker of wild bird feeders, offers a free newsletter on birdfeeding, and bird watching. New subscribers are eligible for a drawing for a free bird feeder.

EcoHealth home.pon.net/ecohealth/pets has a free online newsletter on pet health.

Fat Rat Central mutantspud.com/frc has online information on care and feeding of pet rats plus links to other sources of help.

The Federal Consumer Information Center www.pueblo.gsa.gov has a large assortment of free or low cost pamphlets on a variety of topics including such things as flea control and backyard bird feeding.

Fish N Chips www.reefsuk.org/FishNChips/FNC12-98/FNC12-98.html has an online newsletter for salt water aquarists.

Find a Pet findapet.com/petdirect.htm offers the Pet Direct e-mail newsletter.

Friskies www.friskies.com/frisky_pet.asp has an online e-zine on pet care covering behavior, nutrition and grooming tips, purebred profiles and also promotional offers.

Frog species care sheets are at <u>allaboutfrogs.org/ info/species/index.html</u>

Halo Pets <u>www.halopets.com/holistic.htm</u> offers a complimentary copy of a holistic pet book

Happy Paws <u>www.happy-paws.com/sample.html</u> has an online request for a free booklet "Feeding Your Pet."

Hartz Mountain at <u>www.hartz.com/signup.asp</u> has a free newsletter plus message boards and an online simulator for a "gerbil or hamster" kingdom.

High Hopes Dog Food <u>www.highhopes4pets.com/ hh_free.html</u> has a free quarterly e-mail newsletter.

Guinea Pig Daily Digest <u>w3.ing.unico.it/mail man/listinfo/gpigs</u> has a free newsletter on care of guinea pigs.

Hedgehog Help <u>keremeos.net/hedgehoghobby/ mail-list/index.html</u> has a free mail list for hedge-hog owners who are looking for serious information related to the care, keeping, nutrition, breeding and raising, and general husbandry of the domestic, pet hedgehog.

Herp Care Information Collection www.sonic. net/~melissk/index.html has extensive online information on care of reptiles and amphibians.

ILoveMyPet.com www.ilovemypet.com/news has an online newsletter.

Invisible Fence Co. www.ifco.com/free.htm offers a free magazine for filling out the online form.

The Journal of Animal Physiology and Animal Nutrition has copies of articles at www.blackwell-synergy.com/issuelist.asp?journal=jpn.

Love My Pets.com www.lovemypets.com/ gateway/index.html has a free e-mail newsletter.

Mail Order Pet Supplies at www.mops.on.ca/ newsletter.html has a list of articles about fish.

Merritt Naturals www.merrittnaturals.com/ newsletter/index.cfm is a site for a free newsletter about the absolute nutrition for your dogs and cats.

Nancy's Parrot Sanctuary www.parrot-sanctuary. org/store.html has a free e-mail newsletter.

The Nashville Pet Gazette is a free newsletter distributed to various locations. Check web site for distributors www.thepetgazette.com/find.html.

Pet Bird E-zine www.petbirdreport.com/. While the emphasis of this site is on understanding, preventing and solving behavioral problems in birds, in-depth articles by many knowledgeable writers also cover topics including nutrition, care, breeding, socialization of chicks, weaning, health, ethics, species profiles, product reviews and humor.

Pet Chalet www.petchalet.com/pet_gazette.htm has an online Pet Gazette newsletter.

Pets.com www.pets.com offers an e-mail newsletter.

Pet Directory.com www.petdir.com/petdir maintains an extensive pet directory for pet-related e-zines.

Pet Doc web site at certificate.net/wwio/pets.shtml has free articles, information and an online form to submit questions.

Pet Groomer.com www.petgroomer.com/NEWS LETTER/1098.htm has a free newsletter for pet owners and dog groomers.

Pet Smart www.petsmart.com/misc/pawspective_splash. xshtml has a free newsletter with promotions, shopping deals and contests.

Pets on a Budget at www.stretcher.com/stories/980810a.htm offers a free weekly newsletter on money-stretching ideas.

Pet Owners With AIDS/ARC Resource www.powars.org/html/newsletter.html. This organization plans a newsletter so check the site periodically.

The Pet Station.com web site www.petstation.com/index.html#TOP has online articles of birds, dogs, cats, reptiles, horses and fish plus message boards and a guestbook.

Petstore.com www.petstore.com has a free *Petstories* newsletter.

Petopia at www.petopia.com/default.asp has a free pet care newsletter.

Pet View E-zine www.petview.com/. Sponsored by the National Pet Health & Care Network, this e-zine offers the opportunity to get free expert advice on pet health and behavior.

PetWarehouse.com petswarehouse.com/PetNews
letter.htm has an online Pet Newsletter and a pet
chat room.

Planet Pets planetpets.simplenet.com/index.htm
offers a free monthly Pet Gazette newsletter.

The Pooch Papers. Call: 800-646-4917 for a free
issue of "The Pooch Papers" newsletter.

Purina www.catchow.com offers a free *Pet Life
Magazine* and a free e-mail pet reminder service.

Purina's Silver Pet Program web site www.
silverpets.com has an online form for a free newsletter, information on veterinary savings and food.

Rabbit E-zine www.cyberus.ca/~buntales/. *The
Bunny Thymes* offers information on pet rabbits,
including free veterinarian advice. "Dr. Janet Biggar
and Dr. Anne Downes of Carling Animal Hospital
in Ottawa, Ontario, Canada, both specialize in the
treatment of small animals," and will answer questions on rabbits.

St. Hubers Animal Welfare www.milkbone.com/
library.html has a free e-mail newsletter.

Seminole Feeds www.seminolefeed.com/semi nole_home.html has online newsletters regarding care and feeding of horses.

Snakes as pets are covered with extensive online information at www.ahc.umn.edu/rar/MNAALAS/ Snakes.html.

Sugar Glider Network www.sugarglider.net has extensive online articles on sugar glider care, message boards, links to directories of breeders and vet care; research bibliography and links to scientific studies.

Tetra www.tetra-fish.com has extensive online information on aquarium keeping and a special site for teachers planning an aquarium in their classroom.

Texas Ferret Lovers Club www.texasferret.org/ newsl.html has an online archive to its newsletter *Ferret Footnotes*.

Thompson's Nutritional Technology www. thompsons.com/friends.htm offers a free newsletter to members of its Finicky Friends Club.

!Village Pet www.ivillage.com/pets/features/ petgazette has an online form for an e-mail pet newsletter.

Waggin Tales www.waggintails.com/list.html offers a free catalog and quarterly newsletter.

Wegman's www.wegmans.com/stores/pet/gazette/index.html has a free online Pet Gazette newsletter.

Wellpet at listservice.net/wellpet/subbing.htm offers subscriptions to its member forum.

Winged Wisdom at www.birdsnways.com/wisdom/index.htm#toc is a pet bird e-zine for exotic birds & pet parrots. It includes articles on the care and breeding of pet birds, pet parrots and exotic birds.

Just for Horse Lovers

A listing of horse related publications is at www.horseworlddata.com/regpub.html.

The American Association for Horsemanship Safety www.law.utexas.edu/dawson/index.htm#info has a free information packet. It also has an extensive online library of safety articles available for downloading.

American Miniature Horse Association www.swcp.com/amha/Text/booklet.html offers a free booklet on miniature horses.

Haynet www.haynet.net/Publications has an extensive list of horse-related e-zines.

The Holistic Horse web site www.holistichorse.com/hhnews.html offers a free sample newsletter.

Horse Candy Mall www.horsecandy.com/newsletter.htm offers a free e-mail newsletter.

Horse lovers may order a free quarterly newsletter on horsemanship at www.prairienet.org/horse-sense.

Learn about equine foot care. Go to www.equinevetnet.com/farrier/farrierscience.html which includes the recent articles as well as past articles.

For free articles visit www.thehorse.com and www.thehorse.com/sports_medicine/index.html. They offer tons of sports medicine articles for your horses.

Go to www.icehorse.com for information about the Icelandic horse or go to the Icelandic Horse International for their homepage dedicated to informing owners.

Consult current sites for horse publications, tack and feed supply stores, as well as for information and addresses of breed-specific organizations in which you are interested.

National Plantation Walking Horse Association is found at www.geocities.com/Heartland/Valley/4144/index.html where you can view newsletters and the latest news.

Missouri Fox Trotting Horse Breed Association is found at www.mfthba.com/.

American Saddlebred Horse Association is found online at www.asha.net/.

International Paso Cross Breed Association. Go to www.aeon-systems.com/paso/description.html for information about the Peruvian Paso Horse; aaobpph.org/other_organizations.html has horse associations that include their publications.

American Paint Horse Association has a site at www.apha.com/index.html. It includes an information booth and news and events.

Paso Fino Horse Association www.pfha.org/_vti_bin/shtml.dll/INDEX.HTM.

American Bashkir Curly Registry www.abcregistry.org/theregistry_.htm.

www.horse-previews.com/797articles/american bashkircurly.html is a site that includes an article about this type of horse.

Or visit www.netpets.org/horses/horsclub/horsreg/saddle/horsbshc.html for more information.

American Hanoverian Society-Home page at www.hanoverian.org/.

American Shetland Pony Club—Go to www.horseshoes.com/magazine/shetland/amstpncl.htm to view the *American Shetland Pony Club Journal*.

Free Magazines

Aside from e-zines offered online, there are dozens of excellent print magazines on horses, birds, fish, cats and dogs that will provide you with many hours of entertaining, informative, educational reading. Many publications offer one or more free or sample issues in a trial or introductory subscription offer. If you agree to their offer, they will send you an issue and an invoice for a regular subscription. However, you are not obligated to continue the subscription or pay them any money if, after receiving the samples, you do not wish to continue. You simply write "cancel" on the invoice and send it back to them.

You get to keep the free issues and your only expense is the postage stamp you use to return that first bill.

Nearly every magazine I've ever read has two, three and sometimes as many as four subscription cards inside the pages of copies sold at newsstands and retail outlets. It used to annoy me when these little cards fell out of the pages as I was flipping through the articles, until I realized that these subscription cards often include a free sample or trial offer. Taking advantage of the publishers' generous offers, I began filling them out and sending them in. Within six weeks my sample issues began arriving. When I received an invoice, if I didn't want to continue with my subscription, I wrote "cancel" across it and would not be billed. And if I'm lucky, when I'm at the library, I can often find one of the free sample cards without first buying the magazine from a newsstand (at full cover price).

Listed below are some of the more popular consumer-oriented pet and animal magazines. You can write or call those who do not have web sites for trial subscription information. Many magazines will send a free sample issue upon request but do not publicize that fact.

American Cage-Bird Magazine, 1 Glamore Ct. Smithtown, NY 11787-1851, 516-979-7962.

Arabian Focus Magazine www.arabianfocus.
com/comp.htm offers a complimentary copy of its
magazine.

Avian publications www.avianpublications.com/
magazine.htm has a link to a free 90-day trial for
Bird Times.

Bird Talk has a free 2-month trial subscription
through affiliate.freeshop.com/pg004227.htm

The Cats & Kittens web site www.catsandkittens.
com offers a free trial subscription. Also has links
to subscriptions for *Dog & Kennel* and *Bird Times.*

Cats Magazine www.catsmag.com has a free
online edition and an online subscription form.
Call (800) 829-9125 for a free sample issue.

Dog & Kennel magazine www.dogandkennel.
com/Subscrib.htm has a free trial subscription offer.

Equus Subscription Department, 800-829-5910,
656 Quince Orchard Road, Gaithersburg, MD
20878-1409.

Field Trial Magazine www.fielddog.com/ftm has
an online form for a free trial subscription.

Freshwater and Marine Aquarium. Subscription: Mark Lujan, 144 W. Sierra Madre Blvd., Sierra Madre, CA 91024.

Horse.net www.horsenet.org/mag.htm has an extensive list of horse-related publications that may offer a free sample issue.

Modern Ferret Magazine www.modernferret.com has a free downloadable file, "10 New Tips for Ferret Owners."

Pet Life Magazine has a free trial subscription offer through www.absolutemagazines.com/pet_life. html.

Pets: Part of the Family is offered by Acme Pet acmepet.petsmart.com/registration/indexreg.html. There is an online form for a free 6-month subscription.

Pets Magazine, Subscription Dept. 1300 Don Mills Road, Don Mills, Ontario M3B 3M8 CANADA.

Trail Rider has a free trial subscription offer at www.ncbuy.com/magazines/1186.html. The magazine (www.derbyglass.com/trailrider/) is widely read by recreational horse enthusiasts and has numerous links.

The Western Horseman www.westernhorseman. com/subscriptions/WHsubscribe.htm has some online articles and an online subscription form. Box 7980, Colorado Springs, CO 80933-7980.

NetCent Communications web site, *NC Buy Magazine Store*, at www.ncbuy.com/magazines/ offers free trial offer subscriptions to the following animal-interest magazines. The site includes an online subscription form:

ACK Afield	*AKC Gazette*
Animal Fair	*Animal Market Place*
Animals Exotic and Small Magazine	*Aquarium Fish Magazine*
Bird Talk	*Bird Times*
Cat Fancy	*Cats*
Cats and Kittens	*Dog and Kennel*
Ferrets	*Dog World*
Dog Fancy	*Horse Illustrated*
Pet Life	*Reptiles*

The Animals Agenda   *Trail Rider*

Wild Bird   *Horse and Rider*

Vivariium Magazine (devoted to the care of reptiles and amphibians)

Fancy Publications is a leading publisher of magazines and annuals about pets. They also publish special issues on favorite pets (Popular Breed series) and books (BowTie Press) on the care and training of your pets. Check out the information on their Animal Network web site at www.animalnetwork.com.

In addition to Internet access to pet related material, you can often pick up informative and helpful publications at pet shops, feed stores, pet shows and veterinary clinics. These magazines and newspapers are distributed for free (or you can subscribe and receive them at home) and are supported by individual advertisers. The following is a sampling of a few of the publications found in our area. Check your local pet shops for free magazines covering animal news in your area:

The Pet & Horse Exchange is an all-animal monthly newsletter covering California, Portions of Nevada, Arizona, Hawaii and Canada. It is distributed free at pet stores, feed stores, pet shows, and includes a wide variety of news, announcements and services regarding pets.

The Animal Press is another all-animal publication for Southern California animal lovers. Included are columns, features and news stories along with local advertisements and an animal "Calendar of Events."

Animal House Magazine is a monthly newsletter that looks at animal issues and the personal side of interesting people and their work with animals along with a Pet of the Month and events calendar.

For interesting news and informative articles about all kinds of pets, pick up a free copy of *Pet Care Times* at your local pet store. Articles by well-known authors, veterinarians, and other pet authorities make up this publication.

If you want to buy a horse, *Horsemarket* is a monthly West Coast advertising-supported publication that lists dozens of horses for sale as well as a calendar of horse events and other information.

Today's Horseman is a glossy, monthly magazine that covers the premier equine news market of Southern California. It is chock full of show information, events, dressage news and features.

Pet and Animal Books, Catalogs, Publishers and Bookstores

There are literally thousands of books written about animals and pets. Books have been written about specific breeds of cats, dogs, birds, horses and types of fish. There are wonderful novels on pets. There are historical books on the roles animals have played throughout history. There are books for children and adults alike. There are books on the care and feeding of pets. There are medical books and home veterinary handbooks. And, there are hundreds of books on ways to train your pets.

Building and maintaining a collection of books about the pet(s) you love will allow you to create your own personal library which you can refer to and enjoy for years to come. These books can grow along with your pet and future pet generations. Today, because of the popularity of pet related books (and videos), several publishers specialize in publications about cats, dogs, fish, birds and horses. Often, you can find an ample selection from one well-supplied publisher. Most pet supply catalogs also offer a selection of books and videos.

There are many conveniences associated with shopping from home. With mail-order catalogs you don't have to spend hours running around from place to place looking for a special pet product or book. Ordering by mail gives you the choice of ordering from anywhere and anyone in the country, not just those within driving range.

The following are names of bookstores, book publishers and catalogs that carry or specialize in animal titles and videos. If the company does not have a web site with an e-mail form for requesting a catalog, then write or call and ask for their current catalog. Once you've received their information, you can compare prices (don't forget shipping and handling charges), brands and select from suppliers with the best prices. Often, as a special promotion, they will put a select group of titles on sale and you can save even more off their prices.

Alpine Publications www.alpinepub.com offers a free catalog. Completing an online form enters you into a drawing for a free book.

Amazon.com www.amazon.com has discounts on a very large selection of pet books.

Animal Health Express, 4439 N. Highway Drive., Bldg. 2, Tuscon, AZ 85705-1909. 800-533-8115. Veterinary care books and animal training and care videos.

Avian Publications www.avianpublications.com has an online list of bird books and an online form to receive a free catalog.

The Bookery.com www.thebookery.com/Bookstore/list.cfm/Recommended/Pets.htm.

The Book Stable www.bookstable.com. Call 800-274-2665 or send an e-mail request for a free catalog. This magazine service offers subscriptions to more than 40 horse magazines, in addition to books and videos. Write for a catalog of all titles.

Bowtie Press www.dogfancy.com/bowtie/default.asp, a subsidiary of *Dog Fancy* magazine.

Canine Cornucopia at www.corsini.co.uk/cornucopia/irishter.htm. This is an English specialist in out of print books who also sells to the U.S. market. Has online catalog.

Chazhound www.chazhound.com/books.html.

Catsbuzz members.aol.com/catsbuzz/STORE.htm has over 2,000 cat-related titles.

Dog Lovers Bookshop www.dogbooks.com/index.htm, P.O. Box 117, Gracie Station, New York, NY 10028 212-369-7554.

Dogwise at www.dogandcatbooks.com has thousands of books on dogs and an online form for a free catalog.

Direct Book Services, PO Box 2778, Wenatchee, WA 98807, 800-776-2665. Send for free dog book catalog. Thousands of titles on every subject. New and out of print titles. Videos.

Doral Publishing www.doralpub.com/, 10452 Palmeras Drive, Suite 225 West Sun City, AZ 85373. 1-800-633-5385.

Equine Research Inc. www.equine-research-inc.com has an online book and video store plus an online form to request a free catalog.

Fazo-Corp. Products, Box 69007 RAM, Laval, Quebec H7X 3M2 Canada. Sells cat books. Many titles discounted. Write for catalog.

Fish Link Central www.fishlinkcentral.com/bookstore/index.htm has books about aquarium keeping.

HDW Enterprises and Foothill Felines www.hdw-inc.com/felinebookstore1e.HTM has an online book store for cat lovers.

Howell Book House Co. 1633 Broadway, New York, NY 10019-6708. Tel: 212-654-8458. Specializes in dog breed books.

Jeffers Pet Catalog www.jefferspet.com (1-800-JEFFERS) has a wide variety of books, videos and pet-care items. Check the web site for weekly specials and if you order online you will always get something free.

Leerburg Video leerburg.com. PO Box 218 I, Menomonie, WI 54751. Tel: 715-235-6502. Dog training videos. Personal protection, police, basic obedience, puppy training, tracking. Write or use web site e-mail for a free catalog.

Parrot House Book Store www.parrothouse.com/bookmenu.html.

The Pet Bookshop, PO Box 507, Oyster Bay, NY 11771, 516-922-1169. Extensive line of books covering parrots, dogs, cats, reptiles and fish. Write for catalog.

Pet Expo at www.pet-expo.com/breedbooks.htm has discount dog books.

Pet Remedies.com www.petremedies.com/No Frames/order.html is offering a free 21 day trial offer on *The Doctor's Book of Home Remedies for Dogs and Cats* and has a free 21 day trial offer.

Pet Station petstation.com/bookstor.html is an online bookstore selling a large variety of pet books.

PetsWarehouse.com petswarehouse.com/PetBook. htm has discounted online books.

Planet Pets planetpets.simplenet.com/books. htm has an extensive index of books that may be ordered online.

The Practice Ring. Call: 1-800-553-5319. Exclusively equine titles for every equine interest: horse care, keeping, riding, training, children's books, adult fiction, etc. Free catalog.

Powells Boostore www.powells.com, one of the largest independent bookstores in the country, has thousands of titles of new and used books about pets of all kinds.

R.C. Steele www.rcsteele.com. Online form to request free catalog. Dog equipment and kennel supply catalog. Discount prices. Hundreds of titles on training, care and breeding of dogs. Also has titles on fish, small animals, birds, horses and cats. Most publishers represented.

Robin Bledsoe, Bookseller, bookmarque.net/abaa links.cfm?Dealer=bledsoe. E-mail rbledsoe@world. std.com for catalog query. Hundreds of old, new and imported books on horses.

Silvio Mattacchione & Co. www.silvio-co.com/store/store.htm. Canine library from Canadian specialty publisher. Has online catalog.

T.F.H. Publications, Inc. Publishes books on cats, dogs, birds, fish and small animals www.nylabone.com/bookstore/bookstoreframeset.htm.

J. N. Townsend Publishing, 12 Greenleaf Drive, Exeter, NH 03833. Tel: 603-778-9883. E-mail: JNTown@aol.com. Books about living with animals. Also, nature and country living. Catalog available.

CHAPTER 6

Mail-Order Shopping for Your Pet

If I had to choose, I would rather have birds than airplanes.
—Charles A. Lindberg

As we mentioned in the last chapter, ordering pet supplies through the mail is a convenience that can save you both time and money. Shopping by mail (or online) is more than just filling out an order form, clicking on a web site or calling an 800-phone number. If your goal is to shop by mail or online and save, be prepared to spend some time comparing prices, selection, shipping and handling costs, sales tax, quality, etc.

Recently I bought an orthopedic foam bed with a washable sheepskin cover for my 12-year old English

Springer Spaniel through the mail. I knew that this type of bed was going to cost around $50, having seen it at my neighborhood pet store. Since it was a fairly expensive item, I decided it was worthwhile to do some comparison shopping. I called several pet stores in my area that carried the same bed. Their prices ranged from $50–$78. I also looked through pet supply catalogs, advertisements in pet magazines and on the Internet. I found the exact bed I wanted, on sale, for $35.

However, the catalog required a $50 minimum order. Being the owner of three dogs, I had no trouble finding a couple of other items (also on sale). Since the catalog company was out-of-state, I did not pay sales tax. Here's how my savings added up:

Catalog	Price	Store Price
Dog Bed	$35.00	$50.00
Yard Spray	7.00	15.00
Expandable Leash	10.00	20.00
Shipping. Etc.	7.50	—
Sales Tax	—	3.50
Total Paid	**$59.50**	**$88.50**

I saved $29.00 by ordering the items I needed through a catalog.

General Catalogs

Pet Catalogs—A comprehensive list of toll free numbers for free pet related catalogs can be found at users.snip.net/~carm74/catalog.htm.

Mail Order Pet Shop—800366-7387. 250 Executive Drive Brentwood, NY 11717. 631-595-1717. Web site: www.mopetshop.com. They carry every major manufacturer of pet supplies. Free Catalog.

Upco—800-254-8726P.O. Box 969, St. Joseph, MO 64502, 816-233-8800. Web site: www.upco.com/. Quality bird, dog, cat and horse supplies. Free catalog.

Omaha Vaccine Company—800-367-4444. 3030 L. St., Omaha, NE 68107. 402-731-9600. Web site: www.omahavaccine.com. Supplies for dogs, cats, other house pets and horses.

Pet Usa—P.O. Box 128 Topsail, MA 01983. 800-473-8872, (800-4-PETUSA).

Pet Warehouse—800-443-1160. Web site: www.petwhse.com. Bird, fish, cat, dog supply catalog. Free catalog.

JB Wholesale Pet Supplies—5 Rartlan Rd., Oakland, NJ 07436. 800-526-0388 or Fax 800-788-5005. www.jbpet.com/cgi-bin/main.cgi?page=index2.html.

Pet Accessories—www.valleyvet.com. This free catalog offers a complete pet catalog featuring gift items, clippers, scissors, dryers, brushes, shampoos, vaccines, wormers, rawhide, treats, flea and tick insecticides, collars, toys, kennel equipment, leashes, training equipment, carriers, beds, travel dog beds, and more. Free shipping is available on most items. Free overnight shipping is available on some vaccines.

Animal Health Express—4439 N. Highway Dr., #2, Tucson, AZ 85705-1909. 800-533-8115. Fax 800-437-9898. Quality supplies for livestock, farm animals, cats and dogs. Also contains a tack section. Warehouse direct prices. Free catalog.

Ferret Products—www.ferretstore.com. Finding a site dedicated solely to ferrets is not easy. This site offers free shipping with purchase of $10 or more. The online store offers all types of products for ferrets including, medicines, toys, accessories, grooming supplies and more.

Bird Supply Catalogs

Stromberg's Chicks & Gamebirds—P.O. Box 400, Pine River, MN 56474. 212-587-2222. 800-720-1134. Web site: www.strombergschickens.com. Aviary sets, books and supplies. Catalog on request.

The Feather Farm, Inc.—1181 Fourth Ave., Napa, CA 94559. 707-255-8833. www.featherfarm.com/. Metal nest boxes for bird breeders. Free catalog.

Discount Bird & Reptile Supplies—19640 Sherman Way, Reseda, CA 91335. 818-343-1040. Cages, books, toys, boxes, health products, feed, crocks, etc. Request mail-order catalog.

Lake's Minnesota Macaws, Inc.—639 Stryker Ave., St. Paul, MN 55107. 800-634-2473. Maintenance, breeding and baby bird formulas. Write for brochure.

Inglebrook Forges Quality Cages—2001 East Gladstone Street, Suite D, Glendora, CA 91740. 626-599-0933, 909-599-0933, Fax: 626-599-0933. Bird cage manufacturers. Free catalog.

Advanced Avian Designs—790 Hwy. 105, Suite F, Palmer Lake, CO 80133. 888-408-4967. Web site: www.parrotgyms.com/. Original creations in outdoor bird gyms, parrot sound-n-shake puzzles, toys, etc. Send for free catalog with price list.

Parrots Treasure—PO Box 445, St Louis, MO 63074. 314-770-1148. Handcrafted birdtoys from all natural materials. Free catalog.

Emerald Bird Caddy—2254 Silhouette, Dept. A, Eugene, OR 97402. 800-343-6253. Bird stands, perches, books and edible toys. Free color catalog.

Lyon Electric Company—1690 Brandywine Avenue, Chula Vista, CA 91911. 619-216-3400, Fax: 619-216-3434. Web site: www.lyonelectric.com/. Bird incubators, brooders, feeders, books. Free catalog.

Parrot Love—Rt. 2, Crofton Dr., Box 253A, Parsonburg, MD 21849. Handcrafted made-to-chew toys for budgies and macaws. E-mail: MyBC3@aol.com. Send SASE for free catalog.

Parrots Ahoy—52 Leveroni Ct., Novato, CA 94949. 415-492-8279 E-mail: joseph@choicemall.com. Web site: www.choicemall.com/parrotsahoy/.

Fun, colorful and safe toys for every bird at reasonable prices. Free catalog.

Firefly Studios—PO Box 189, Amity, OR 97101. 800-777-9242. Fax: 503-835-0311. Web site: <u>www. fireflypublishing.com/</u>. Artful exotic birds silk-screened in 6 prismatic colors on T-shirts. Free flyer.

Equine/Horse Supply Catalogs

Most of these catalogs also have clothing, equipment, boots, personal tack, etc. for horseback-riders.

Western Wholesalers—PO Box 84, Richardson, TX 75083. 972-671-5955. Fax: 972-671-7566. Web site: <u>www.wholesalesaddles.com/</u>. Free saddle and tack catalog.

State Line Tack, Inc.—PO Box 428, Plaistow, NH 03865. 888-839-9640. Web site: <u>www.state linetack.com/</u>. Discount brand name English and Western riding tack and apparel catalog.

Vapco—360 Merrimack St., Bldg. 5, #23, Lawrence, MA 01843. 978-975-0302. Orders Only 800-523-5614, Fax 978-794-4929. Web site: <u>www.vapco.com</u>. Discount horse feed. Free brochure.

Big D's Harness—9998 State Rt. 43, Streetsboro, OH 44242. 800-321-2142. Web site: www.bigdweb.com/. Horse supplies. Free 100 page catalog.

Horse Health USA—PO Box 9101, Wooster, OH 44711. 330-262-9009, Fax Orders: 330-492-1516. 800-321-0235. Web site: www.pbshorsehealth.com/. Horses supplies. Free catalog.

D.T. Industries—Box 460, Exeter, Ontario NOM 1 SO, Canada. Horse stall and feeding systems. Free product brochure.

Jeffers Vet Supply—1610 Old Airport Road, West Plains, MO 65775. 417-256-3196, 800-633-7592. Web site: www.jefferspet.com/jeffers/. Riding equipment, grooming products, tack room supplies, vaccines, ointments, accessories, etc. (also carries many other pet supplies). Free catalog.

Country Manufacturing, Inc.—PO Box 104, 333 Salem Ave., Fredericktown, OH 43019. 740-694-9926. Fax: 740-694-5088. Web site: www.country mfg.com/. Horse supplies, barn equipment, hay racks, bridle racks, cross ties, lawn and garden.

Wiese Vet Supply—PO. Box 192, Eldon, MO 65026 800-869-4373. Horse supplies, vaccines, equipment, etc. Free 104-page catalog.

Source—101 Fowler Road, N. Branford, CT, 06471. 203-488-6400, Fax: 203-488-6474. 800-232-2365. Web site: www.4source.com/. Macro-nutrients for horses. Free product information.

Parelli Horse-Man-Ship—PO Box 3729, Pagosa Springs, CO 81147. 970-731-9400. 800-642-3335. Fax: 888-731-9722 or 970-731-9722. Web site: www. parelli.com/welcome.htm. Natural horse handling equipment and videos. Free catalog.

Rudl Fence Mfg, Inc.—800-599-RUDL, 800-599-7835 or 908-638-8521. Web site: www.countyonline. com/shopping/ad-rfd.html. Quality wood fencing. Free brochure.

Stockton Supply Co.—800-441-5832. Manufacturers of quality wood and wire fencing. Free brochure.

Suitability—P.O. Box 3244, Chico, CA 95927-3244. 800-207-0256, Fax: 530-899-7128. Web site: www.suitability.com/. Riding apparel and horse equipment sewing patterns. Free catalog.

Vetline Equine—425 John Deere Road, Fort Collins, CO 80524. 970-484-1900, Fax: 970-484-7666, 800-962-4554. Web site: www.vetlineequine. com/. Quality veterinary drugs and supplies for horses. Free catalog.

Head Horse Jumps, Inc.—17956 Foreston Road, Parkton, MD 21120. 410-239-7973. Horse jumps. Free catalog.

Bloodline Vet Supply—800-346-2675. Discount horse supplies. Free catalog.

Breyer—14 Industrial Road, Pequannock, NJ 07440. 973-694-5006, Fax: 973-694-5213. Customer Service 973-633-5090. Web site: www. BreyerHorses.com/. Free color Breyer horse brochure. Send postcard.

Catalogs for Dogs and Cats

Pet Quarters—1 Maplewood Dr., Hazelton, PA 18201. Fax: 570-384-2500. 888-PET-NETT. Web site: www.petquarters.com/cgi-bin/petquarters. store front. Healthcare, training, grooming, fashions, gifts and collectable dog andcat products. Free catalog.

Categorically—Wilkins Road, Durham, NC 27701. 919-71-9722. Best of everything for cats and cat lovers. Free catalog.

Leonine Products—Box 657, Springfield, VT 05156. 802-885-3888. Fabulous feline fun furniture. Free catalog.

R.C. Steele—888-839-9420. Web site: www.
rcsteele.com/. Wholesale dog equipment and kennel
supplies. Free catalog.

Care-A-Lot—1617 Diamond Springs Road,
Virginia Beach, VA 23455. Fax: 757-460-0317. 800-
343-7680. Web site: www.carealot.org/mmastore/
default.asp. Dog and cat supplies.

Tri-Tronics—P.O. Box 17660, Tucson, AZ
85710. Fax: 520-290-0894. 800-456-4343. www.
tritronics.com/. Products for obedience or companion
dogs. (The Tritonics system should only be used
in conjunction with a proper training program.
Please consult with a reputable dog trainer before
proceeding.)

Dog-Master Systems—5096 Wilshire, Box
902347, Palmdale, CA 93590. Puppy and dog
training systems.

Petdoors U.S.A.—4523 30th St. W., Bradenton,
FL 34207. 800-749-9609 or 941-758-1951, Fax:
800-283-8045 or 941-758-0274. Web site: www.
petdoorsusa.com/. Manufacturers of pet doors.

Hale Security Pet Door—5622 N. 52nd Ave., #4,
Glendale, AZ 85301. 800-646-HSPD (4773). Pet
doors and security pet products.

Cat-A-Log—877-CAT-PAWS (228-7297), Fax: 305-754-6558. Web site: www.acatalog.com/ shop/index2.html. Products for cats.

Sporting Dog Specialties—1989 Transit Way, Brockport, NY 14420. 716-352-9160. Everything for training a hunting dog.

Natural Animal—7000 U.S. 1 North, St. Augustine, FL 32095. 800-274-7387. Fax: 904-824-5100. Web site: www.naturalanimal.com/. Natural flea control products. Free catalog.

Cats, Cats, & Cats—P.O. Box 270, Monroe, NY 10950. 914-782-4141. Web site: www.market plaza.com/cats/cats.html. Free color catalog listing various cat products.

International Llama Association—PO Box 1891, Kalispell, MT 59903. 406-257-0282, Fax 406-257-8780. Web site: www.internationalllama.org/. Free catalog. A complete source of information on breeders, videos and publications, gift items, llama insurance, packers, products and services.

Incats—Redwood City, CA 94063. 650-851-5890. Original quality Hanes silkscreened T-shirts/ sweats. Free brochure.

Gallery of Cats—1800 S. Robertson Blvd., Bldg. 6, #403, Los Angeles, CA 90035-4352. 818-782-5740. Web site: www.dreamtek.com/gallery-of-cats/. Free catalog of outstanding cat items by cat loving artists.

Loujon's Gifts—3322 Hwy. 6 South, Sugar Land, TX 77478. 800-730-4228. Web site: www.loujons gifts.com/. Collectible figurines. Thousands of dog and cat figures. Over 70 breeds. Free catalog.

Dogs By the Yard—P.O. Box 341, Portsmouth, RI 02871. Unique animal design fabrics and novelty items. Catalog $1.

Walnut Miniatures—Box 245, Barnegat Light, NJ 08006. 609-494-2096. Cat stickers, decals, iron-ons, T-shirts, sweatshirts, gifts.

CHAPTER 7

Still More Ways to Save

The better I get to know men, the
more I find myself loving dogs . . .
—Charles de Gaulle

In addition to the savings we have shown you for products and services for your pets, there are also a number of overlooked and little known sources of bargains and gifts of which many people are unaware.

For example, did you know that there are dozens of contests, competitions and sweepstakes each year that award free products and cash prizes to winning pets and their owners? Pet food manufacturers, especially, run contests to help promote their products. Prizes for winning pets range from collars and grooming supplies to a year's supply of pet food and feature parts in upcoming movies and television shows. Prizes for pet owners include stuffed animals, appliances, vacations and cash awards.

Attend a Pet Show

Pet shows are one of the most interesting and entertaining events we know of that offer fun for the whole family. Besides the many cat and dog shows sponsored by kennel clubs and pet food manufacturers, there are turtle and tortoise shows, live amphibian and reptile exhibits and numerous bird shows. Sometimes manufacturers and pet organizations combine efforts and get together to sponsor shows. America's Family Pet Show is an enormous show produced at the Los Angeles Country Fair Grounds and features several buildings of exhibits and thousands of birds, cats, dogs, fish, reptiles, turtles, chickens, miniature horses, goats and other small animals.

In addition to the animals on display at these pet shows and expositions, there are demonstrations, product and pet services exhibits and seminars. But what we come for are the free samples and mountains of information that exhibitors give away to attendees. We usually come away from a typical pet show with several shopping bags worth of sample and trial size products, from dog and cat food to vitamins and flea shampoo. Some manufacturers will give as much as 5 and 10 lb. bags of their latest pet food formulas.

You can find out about upcoming shows through announcements in the events or calendar listing of your newspaper. In our area two of the largest newspapers, *The Los Angeles Times* and *The Daily News*, both have weekly detailed lists of upcoming events for pets, including club shows, vaccination clinics, obedience classes and "open houses" for adoption. Pet stores also have flyers on upcoming events. Many radio and television stations also have community calendar segments on which pet show listings may be posted. Web sites that include listings for pet shows are: www.planetpets. simplenet.com/petshows.htm and www.showevent. com/Pet%20show%20news.htm. Most major pet shows are listed several months in advance in the leading pet magazines (available at libraries and sold in pet stores). Check out the next show coming to your area and start collecting those freebies.

Contests and Freebies

The following web sites contain information of interest to pet owners, including contests, shows, competitive events, free downloads, online games, chat rooms and bulletin boards. FAQs on health, training and care of pets and e-mail queries of vets and other pet professionals are also available. The United States Dog Agility Association, PO Box 850955, Richardson, TX 75085-0955. 214-231-9700.

Web site: www.dogpatch.org/agility/ and www.usdaa. com/news.htm#TOP. Both web sites have information on the Pedigree Grand Prix of Dog Agility for dogs of all sizes, purebreds and mixed breeds. Qualifying events take place in 18 regions. Participants must navigate a timed obstacle course that includes weaving through poles, scaling ramps and racing through tunnels. This web site has links to dog agility clubs. Check web site periodically for Dog Obedience and Agility championships www.woofs. org/puperoni/index.htm.

This site has links to dog obedience trials, events and competitions www.dogpatch.org/obed/. The Rolling Hills Wildlife Center offers an animal conservation newsletter www.rhrwildlife.com/newspg4. htm.

Go here to find information for dog shows in Canada www.compupets.com/westerndogshows/ index2.htm.

Dog World Magazine maintains listings for AKC dog shows www.dogworldmag.com/show/akcshows.html.

Now you can download the first ever screen saver developed for cats at www.petsource.com/whiskas/ pages/screen.htm. This screen saver will amuse your cat while protecting your monitor when it is not in use. Also available for download is the very first commercial made entirely with cats in mind. It features a series of feline-focused sounds and images. A link to another Petsource page offers free dog screensavers, interactive games and other free educational materials that can be downloaded. Also on the web site are postings of the winners in the Whiskas drawing contest.

Hills Science Diet offers coupons and other information of interest to pet owners upon completion of an online survey. Hills picks a "Pet of the Month" for posting on the web site www.hillspet. com/public/about/form.html.

Win a one-of-a-kind Friskies Cat Tower in the Friskies pet food sweepstakes. Five Grand prize packages, $10,000 value; 10 first prize packages www.friskies.com/sweeps.asp.

This site is the event manager for the Friskies ALPO Canine Frisbee disc Championships. These contests consist of Local Championships and Regional Championships which culminate in the World Championship. Site has an online form to receive Training Guide & Schedule www.skyhoundz. com/competition.html.

The Friskies Grand Gourmet Sweepstakes is no longer held but the cat food site does offer several

free offers and coupons <u>www.friskies.com/fr/</u>
<u>fr_so_intro.html</u>.

The makers of Jerky Treats and Meaty Bones
offers a free screensaver on their web site <u>www.</u>
<u>jerkytreats.com/</u>.

The National Committee for Dog Agility, 401
Bluemont Circle, Manhattan, KS 66052 runs a similar
contest to the U.S. Dog Agility Association's.

The Pedigree Challenge Series offers winning
UKC Beagles a large variety of prizes, including 880
pounds of Pedigree dog food <u>www.ukcdogs.com/</u>
<u>events/pc2000.html</u>.

The Ashley Whippet Invitational goes all the
way up to the international level of competition.
For information write Ashley Whippet Invitational,
PO Box 16279, Encino, CA 91416. <u>www.ashley</u>
<u>whippet.com/</u>.

ScoopAway Kitty litter holds a new contest for
free kitty litter every month <u>www.scoopaway.com/</u>
<u>adventure/</u>.

Pro Plan Sweepstakes—Monthly winner receives
a year's supply of pet food <u>www.proplen.com/</u>
<u>hpframeset.asp:Mode=Dog</u>. Special offers from

ALPO are at this web site. The offers change throughout the year, so remember to come back and see what's new!

Fancy Feast cat food has periodic special offers at this web site. www.friskies.com/ff/ff_so_intro.html.

The Tidy Cat web page has links to coupon offers and free film, as well as free wallpaper and screensaver downloads www.tidycat.com/filler/productinfo.cfm.

Kibbles-n-Bits has online registration for coupon offer and provides a free plug in to allow you to generate coupons on your own printer www.kibbles-n-bits.com/coupon.htm.

Cycle Dog Food has a free poster with purchase of dog food. See site for details www.cycledog.com/promos.htm.

Heinz Pets offers a free "Snausages" screensaver at www.snausages.com/saver.htm and a free "Pounce" screensaver at www.pouncecat.com/pfun.htm.

Pets @ Play's toll free number 1-800-719-3890 provides free e-mail question and answer service with veterinarian Dr. Brent Jackson. Questions can also be submitted to "Paws," the site mascot www.ilovemypet.com/askus.html.

At the Action Cat web site you can find free online games, free e-postcards with animal themes, and links to other pet-related sites www.actioncat. com/contents.html.

The South Florida.com web site offers free programs for pet owners including Pet Veterinary Records, dog and cat cursors and computer games. They also offer free e-mail updates for pet contests in Southern Florida, pet events and features www.sofla. com/living/pets/pet_contest.html.

The Palm Beach Interactive web site offers a free pet calendar that can be downloaded, as well as links to pet related web search engines and links to other pet and animal organizations in the southern Florida area www.gopbi.com/living/pets/pet_contest.html.

The South Paw Pet Catalog online site provides an e-mail question and answer service with a veterinarian plus extensive FAQs. They also conduct ongoing contests and have an extensive archived question and answer section. Great links to web sites of non-profit animal advocacy groups and organization are also featured www.southpawpets. com/index.htm.

Martin Pet Foods provides information on nutrition, pet feeding www.marpet.com/contest.html. Enter their pet contest via e-mail or by sending a photo and a story of your pet to Pet Corner Contest, Gifts Galore, 1323 Miller Drive, Los Angeles, CA 90069.

The site www.giftsgalore.com/pet/ramroswin.html includes excerpts from Pet Healthy Cookbook, addresses and phone numbers of animal advocacy groups, and they post free online newsletter.

Here's a contest sponsored by Advantage Flea Control. They're looking for "singing pets" to appear in Advantage flea control commercials. The winner receives $1,000, a year's supply of Advantage flea control from their veterinarian and a recording studio session www.nofleas.com/sing/sing.html.

Pet Jewelry Beverly Hills, PO Box 87448, Phoenix, AZ 85080 Tel: 602-978-5860. Offers free e-mail reminder service for vaccinations. There are also FAQs and information on animal health pet jewlery.com/.

Orange County Now.com has a monthly pet contest for residents of Orange County, CA. They offer free "ani-mail" e-mail update and links to other Orange County pet and animal sites www.ocnow. com/living/pets/contest.html.

CBC4KIDS, CBC Radio, Box 500, Station A, Toronto, Ontario M5W 1E6 will post pictures of kids pets free of charge, and they pick one for "Pet of the Month" honors www.cbc4kids.ca/general/ kids-club/pet-arena/default.html.

A site sponsored by the Kentucky Humane Society, 241 Steedly Drive, Louisville, KY 40214, (502) 366-3355, has a free online game and coloring page www.win.net/~kyhumane/welcome.html.

My Montana.com provides links to a variety of animal-related web sites for products and services directory.montana.com/Shopping/Pets/.

Dogskills Academy offers a free weekly e-mail newsletter on dog behavior modification as well as a free gift for completing an online survey, free reports on a variety of dog training issues, and a free week of online dog training for recommending a friend to sign up for their e-mail newsletter www. solvingdogproblems.com/.

The Bulldog Store, 6 Barnaby Lane, Hartsdale, NY 10530, 800-654-9790, has free online game and periodic contests for bulldog owners and their pets www.bulldogstore.com/games.html.

Internetpets.com 877-414-PETS (7387) conducts an on-going "pet of the month" contest. The winner receives a special gift collection. The site also offers a free pet care newsletter and free veterinary advice www.internetpets.com/newsletter/petofthemonth.html.

DogFriendly.com offers free online e-mail, and links to various free online pet-related magazines and newsletters. They have an on-going monthly contest for free pet-related items and online entry for various monthly contests. Also, six entrants per month win a free bag of Buddy Biscuits Cookie Mix sponsored by Cloud Star PO Box 14437, San Luis Obispo, CA 93406, 800-361-9079 www.dogfriendly. com/mysearch/dogportal.html.

Iams Company offers online registration which makes participants eligible for a drawing for a year's supply of free Eukanuba Dog or Cat Food, with a total of four winners per year. Once you are registered, Iams will keep you posted about pet news and nutrition information with regular e-mails. You'll also be eligible to receive special offers good towards Eukanuba and Iams Dog & Cat Foods. The Iams Company, 7250 Poe Avenue, Dayton, Ohio 45414; Phone: 800-525-4267 www.iams.com/register/index.asp.

Regal Pet Foods Breeder Program——Call 800-638-7006 or e-mail the company when you whelp a litter.

Each puppy gets a free 4-lb. bag of Regal Puppy Bites, and a copy of "Your New Puppy" booklet. Send in the name, address, and phone number of each new puppy owner, and Regal will send a $5.00 voucher good on any Regal formula. That's $5.00 per new puppy. Example: 5 puppies = $25.00 in vouchers. Each new puppy owner becomes part of Regal's mailing program, and will get several mailings during that first and most important year of growth. These mailings will contain educational information and generous coupons. Send puppy information to: Regal Pet foods, PO Box 216, Lutherville, Maryland 21094 www.regalpetfoods. com/html/dogframe.html.

Wysong offers a free subscription to the "thinking persons" E-mail newsletter. Short, periodic e-mail postings containing provocative thoughts, new research findings, resources, new products, humor, health-related news and more. Send e-mail to Wysong@tm.net and say "Subscribe" — easy to unsubscribe too. Subscribers e-mail will not be sold or given out to others www. wysong.net/.

The Dog Bone Club offers a free newsletter members.aol.com/dogboneclub/home.htm.

Lists of Alpo Canine Frisbee Disc Championship events can be found at ashleywhippet.com/ reopenevents.htm.

Dial-a-Pet Hotline

There are now several "help hotlines" available for pet owners with questions about a variety of subjects: Hill's Pet Products has a toll-free help line for dog and cat owners with questions about the nutrition and feeding behavior of pets. Call 800-445-5777 between 8 a.m. and 5 p.m. (CST) to speak with one of their dietary management consultants. Answers to computerized questions are provided 24 hours a day. Hill's Pet Products has a web site at www.hillspet.com.

In the event your dog has been poisoned, help is available through the ASPCA National Animal Poison Control Center which is administered through the University of Illinois, College of Veterinary Medicine. Callers can either call a toll-free line, (800) 548-2423 and pay $45 per case (charged to a credit card) or (900) 680-0000 and the $45 will be billed to their telephone number. (The charges are necessary to supplement funding of the program.) www.napcc.aspca.org/.

The CompuServe Pets/Animal Forum is an online computer service where pet owners and professionals from around the world can communicate with each other. Pet lovers can talk, compare notes, give and receive advice and swap stories about their pets. The Pets/Animal Forum is divided into several sections, each led by a professional in the field to help answer questions and concerns. Forums available include Vendors, Kids 'n' Pets, Animals, Aquaria/Fish, Horses, Dogs and Vet care www.compuserve.com/gateway/default.asp.

CHAPTER 8

Organizations and Associations

*I am in favor of animals' rights as
well as human rights. That is the
way of the whole human being.*
—Abraham Lincoln

Over the past 15 years pet owners have taken a
much more active role in choosing the best health
care products and services for their pets. In keeping
up with this demand, the pet product marketplace
has grown by leaps and bounds, now offering a
wide variety of premium pet food and health care
products wisely targeted at the growing number of
concerned pet owners who want only the very best
for their pet. This increased awareness concerning
animal well being is also reflected in the vast number of animal welfare agencies found throughout
the world today.

As a compassionate pet owner, you probably care about all animals, from stray cats and dogs to orphaned farm animals and endangered wildlife. For this reason you should know that there are more associations and organizations dedicated to providing animals with a better quality of life than ever before.

While government-operated shelters are commonly found throughout the U.S., there are also numerous privately run, non-profit associations concerned with animal welfare. These organizations have varied objectives, but all are dedicated to protecting animal rights by eliminating animal cruelty and exploitation and providing the public with information about animal care and control. A large number of these groups offer shelter for unwanted animals (and many elect not to resort to euthanasia), while others feature low-cost spay and neutering clinics as well as animal care education seminars. Some groups are also quite active in demonstrating against institutions that use animals for medical research. Most groups also publish leaflets, brochures or newsletters on their web sites that provide valuable animal care data for anyone concerned.

You also might be interested to know that many of these groups rely on a strong volunteer program. If you donate your time at a local agency, you might assist in caring for the animals at the shelter or helping abandoned animals find a warm and loving home. Many people find it a rewarding experience to serve in their community. As a pet owner and someone who cares about animals, you may want to contact some of the organizations listed below for further information.

Humane Society of the United States
2100 L Street, NW
Washington, DC 20037
202-452-1100
www.hsus.org/

With over 800,000 members nationwide, this group is one of the largest animal welfare organizations in the country. Their overall goal is to prevent cruelty to animals, accomplished through public education, legislative lobbying and taking legal action against irresponsible pet owners, caretakers and breeders. This organization is also opposed to hunting and trapping and the use of animals for medical research. Moreover, they monitor zoos and animal exhibits for any sign of inhumane treatment and strive to protect endangered species and marine mammals. With eight regional groups in the U.S., this group is an ideal source for learning more about responsible pet care, how to reduce animal overpopulation and eliminate animal suffering. The web site contains a long list of free resources, including shelters, adoption services and e-zines.

International Fund for Animal Welfare
411 Main Street
Yarmouth Port, MA 02675
508-744-2000
www.ifaw.org/

This group is quite well known for working closely with other national and international animal welfare agencies in promoting public education and support concerning the prevention of cruelty to animals, saving endangered species and reducing animal suffering.

American Society for the Prevention of Cruelty to Animals (ASPCA)
441 E. 92nd Street
New York, NY 10128
212-876-7700
www.aspca.org/

Founded in 1866, the ASPCA is one of the nation's oldest animal welfare agencies. In protecting and promoting animal rights, they manage hundreds of animal adoption shelters throughout the U.S., offer low cost spay and neutering services, work through legal channels to implement new animal protection laws and provide various public information seminars on the prevention of cruelty to animals as well as the importance of compassionate and humane animal treatment.

Fund for Animals
200 W. 57th Street
New York, NY 10019
212-246-2096
www.fund.org/

Originators of the popular bumper sticker, "We Speak for Those Who Can't," the Fund for Animals works to protect both wild and domestic animals from cruelty, suffering and endangerment. Their concerns range from saving dolphins exploited by tuna fishermen to seeking more humane treatment of greyhound racing dogs and eliminating medical experiments performed on animals. They often take legal action to protect and publicize inhumane animal treatment.

Animal Protection Institute of America
2831 Fruitridge Rd.
Sacramento, CA 95820
916-731-5521
www.api4animals.org
E-mail: onlineapi@aol.com

Dedicated to advancing humane animal treatment, this agency produces documentaries, publishes informative newsletters and campaigns for animal rights legislation. Concerned with both wild and domestic animals, they educate the public about such topics as the prevention of pet overpopulation, the unethical use of leg-hold traps, the killing of marine mammals and the decline of endangered species.

They also actively demonstrate in protest against inhumane animal treatment institutions. Membership is $15.00 annually. Members receive a quarterly magazine.

National Humane Education Society (NHES)
521-A East Market Street
Leesburg, Virginia 20176
703-777-8319
www.nhes.org/index.html

This well-known agency is devoted to fighting animal cruelty and protecting wildlife. Unlike some groups, the National Humane Education Society operates animal care facilities that are dedicated to the permanent care of lost, sick or abandoned animals. They enforce animal rights laws already in place and seek new animal protection laws. Additionally, they promote sterilization of pets to prevent overpopulation, conduct seminars and present films to better educate the public about animal welfare.

Massachusetts Society for the Prevention of Cruelty to Animals
350 South Huntington Ave.
Boston, MA 02130
617-522-7400
mspca.org/

As the second oldest animal welfare agency in the nation, founded in 1868, this group operates three large animal hospitals and eight animal shelters throughout the state. They have a legislative department that monitors animal protection bills and lobbies for animalrights. The organization employs 13 uniformed animal control officers who are responsible for investigating animal cruelty allegations and inspecting animal exhibits and institutions. They also work to inform the public about animal welfare through various educational programs.

Friends of Animals National Headquarters
777 Post Road
Darien, CT 06820
203-656-1522
www.friendsofanimals.org/

The fundamental goal of Friends of Animals is to educate the public about the danger of pet overpopulation and the need for sterilization. They offer low-cost spay and neutering certificates redeemable at over 1,300 veterinary hospitals across the country. To purchase a discount certificate, call 1-800-321-PETS. This group operates using a large percentage of volunteers and takes an active stand against unethical animal practices such as leg-hold traps and animal slaughter for consumption or fur apparel.

Associated Humane Societies
124 Evergreen Ave.
Newark, NJ 07114
973-824-7080
www.petfinder.org/shelters/NJ01.html
With three different offices in New Jersey, this organization features complete animal care centers with medical services and an adoption program for unwanted animals. It actively pursues animal rights legislation, presents educational programs at schools and sponsors various projects as well as running the Popcorn Park Zoo, PO Box 43, Humane Way, Forked River, NJ 08731, 609-693-1900. Numerous animal rights and advocacy groups are listed at this web site: www.veganism.co.uk/organs.htm.

Morris Animal Foundation
45 Inverness Drive, E.
Engelwood, CO 80112
800-243-2345
www.MorrisAnimalFoundation.org/
This group brings together different animal organizations and individuals concerned with the health problems of domestic and zoo animals. It sponsors medical research studies focusing on assorted health problems and works to improve basic animal health standards. The web site lists postings for various events, it holds seminars on animal health care and it also posts articles on animal health issues.

Animal Rights Mobilization
P.O Box 805859
Chicago, IL 60680
773-381-1181
www.animalrts.org
e-mail: kayarm@earthlink.net

A national grass roots organization with a network of more than 100 local groups, this organization works to publicize inhumane treatment of animals, especially cases dealing with large-scale institutionalized abuses of animals. They are active in legal protest demonstrations, legislative campaigns for animal rights and offer educational programs, including a film series, to the public.

The Delta Society
P.O. Box 1080
Renton, WA 98057-1080
206-226-7357
www.deltasociety.org/

The focus of this group is to dispense information on the importance of human and animal bonding, which can be spiritually, emotionally and physically uplifting. As an information resource center, they help establish guidelines for animal visitation programs to such places as nursing homes, handicap clinics and hospitals. They founded the Pet Partners program in which pet owners take their pets to visit lonely and/or disabled people. All of the animals in this program have passed the Good Canine Citizen Test which is monitored by American Kennel Club affiliates throughout the country. The test states that the animal has a good disposition and a clean bill of health.

International Society for Animal Rights
965 Griffin Pond Road
Clarks Summit, PA 18411
800-543-ISAR; 570-586-2200
i-s-a-r.com/aboutISAR.htm

This group is primarily concerned with preventing animal exploitation and abuse. They coordinate demonstrations against animal abuse in institutions, formulate new laws protecting animals, take up legal issues that address animal rights and sponsor educational conferences.

In Defense of Animals
131 Camino Alto, Suite E
Mill Valley, CA 94941-2254
415-388-9641
www.idausa.org
E-mail: ida@idausa.org

Concerned with inhumane animal treatment, In Defense of Animals is committed to protecting wildlife, promoting non-animal research and taking legal action to assist in animal rights issues. They frequently organize demonstrations at institutions that use animals for research experimentation and attempt to rescue animals exploited in this manner. They also publish a quarterly newsletter on animal rights and maintain an animal abuse hot line.

American Humane Association
63 Inverness Drive. E.
Engelwood, CO 80112
800-227-4645
www.amerhumane.org/

As an umbrella organization representing different agencies and individuals, this group strives to educate the public about animal cruelty prevention and basic animal care and training. They work to raise the standard of quality at many shelters and advocate reducing the use of euthanasia by finding better alternatives. Concerned about protecting both wild and domestic animals, they take an active role in lobbying for new animal rights legislation, oversee the treatment of animals used in television and film and provide educational programs.

American Anti-Vivisection Society
801 Old York Road # 204
Jenkintown, PA 19046-1685
215-887-0816
www.aavs.org/

Founded in 1883, this organization greatly opposes all practices of vivisection (cutting open or operating on live animals, usually under anesthesia, for the purpose of medical experimentation). They publish pamphlets educating the public about animal vivisection and use their funds to sponsor research on vivisection alternatives. They offer several free booklets you can receive by sending them a postcard. Examples of publications include: *A Guide For Eliminating Pound Seizure*, *Why We Oppose Vivisection*, and *The Case Book of Experiments with Living Animals*, which details horrifying case histories of how animals are used for medical experimentation.

> Animal Legal Defense Fund
> 127 Fourth Street
> Petaluma, CA 94952
> 707-769-7771
> www.aldf.org
> E-mail info@aldf.org

The Animal Legal Defense Fund is made up of attorneys who lend their expertise to animal rights issues. They offer a network referral listing of attorneys throughout the U.S. who will assist animal rights activists and associations seeking legal representation. They maintain a library concerning judicial cases relevant to animal welfare issues.

American Veterinary Medical Association
930 N. Meacham Road
Schaumburg, IL 60196
847-925-8070
www.avma.org/
E-mail: avmainfo@avma.org

This association is made up of over 50,000 professional animal health practitioners, including those who work with livestock, lab animals and small domestic animals. They educate the public about important animal health care information through educational programs, films, videos and press releases. They also provide members with insurance programs covering health, life and malpractice. Together with the American Animal Hospital Association, they established the observance of the National Pet Week (each year in May) with the motto "Happiness Is a Healthy Pet."

American Animal Hospital Association
www.healthypet.com/index.html

Members of this organization are all small animal veterinarians from the U.S., Canada and various other countries. The association works to keep its members up to date on medical breakthroughs and on top of management techniques through various educational programs. Members can either be a practitioner affiliate or they can have their clinic critically evaluated to be certified under the standards established by the association. They offer free copies of booklets and circulars.

Cat Rescue Group

www.rescuers.com/cat.htm

This web site has extensive listings for cat rescue groups and shelters in California.

The Cat Fanciers' Association Inc.

PO Box 1005

Manasquan, NJ 08736-0805

732-528-9797

www.cfainc.org/

As the world's largest registry of pedigreed cats, CFA has registered over 1,000,000 cats. In addition, the organization promotes the welfare of cats and the improvement of their breed, licenses cat shows held under the rules of the organization and promotes the interest of breeders and exhibitors of cats. The CFA is also affiliated with the Robert H. Winn Foundation, a non-profit corporation, which supports health-related studies into feline medical problems.

American Cat Fanciers Association

PO Box 203

Point Lookout, MO 65726

417-334-5430

www.acfacat.com/

E-mail: info@acfacat.com

A service association for the registration of pure-bred cats and litters, this international group has members from as far away as Australia, Japan and

Germany. They sponsor pet shows (including a non-breed household cat show), offer certificates of breeding, assist breeders seeking a better strain of purity and work with clubs that put on cat shows.

Note: Refer to Chapter 4, which has additional names and addresses of cat, dog and bird registries and clubs.

American Horse Council
1700 K St., NW, Suite 300
Washington, DC 20006
202-296-4031
www.pet-vet.com/ahc.htm

As a trade association for the horse industry, members include recreational riders, people in the horse industry and those interested in political issues concerning horses. The group lobbies for bills pertaining to equine protection, monitors new tax laws that affect the horse industry and state legislation dealing with zoning changes for horse property. They have five advisory committees which cover such issues as horse shows, health maintenance and horse racing.

American Quarter Horse Association
PO Box 200
Amarillo, TX 79168
806-376-4811
www.aqha.org/index2.html

This organization has over 240,000 members consisting of breeders and others interested in the

American quarter horse. The group registers pedigrees, maintains records and approves shows, contests and races.

Animal Transportation Association
10700 Richmond Avenue, Suite 201
Houston, Texas 77042
713-532-2177
e-mail: AATA@npscmgmt.com

Comprised of companies and individuals that transport animals by air, truck, rail and sea, this international membership organization works to improve the conditions of animal welfare transportation. Most of the members are airlines and freight forwarders, but some breeders also belong. They help regulate the shipment of all types of animals, including domestic, livestock, lab animals and wildlife. For consumers interested in shipping animals, this group offers a resource listing on all their members detailing their animal transportation specialty.

The Pet Food Institute
1200 19th St., NW Suite 300
Washington, DC 20036
202-857-1120
www.pfionline.org/

The Pet Food Institute was organized in 1958 as the national trade association of dog and cat food manufacturers. Industry sponsored public affairs and owner education programs encourage responsible dog and cat ownership. The Institute works closely with veterinarians, humane groups and local animal control officials in order to provide information on pet feeding, training and health care. The PFI provides information at its web site on pet care and training. They also work with humane associations in developing a model pet ordinance outlining eight steps to ensure proper pet care. In addition to distributing hundreds of articles and broadcast announcements on the importance of proper pet care, breeding control, etc., PFI also sponsors research on the human/animal bond that documents the value of pets to people in our society.

Feline Refuge
PO Box 2042
Mt. Pleasant, SC 29465
888-849-2260
www.awod.com/gallery/probono/feline/page2.htmle

The Feline Refuge is in South Carolina and has been successful in reducing the stray population by 20,000 cats and kittens with low cost spay/neuter programs with the help of pro bono veterinarian surgery. Currently the Refuge places 250 vaccinated and sterile animals in loving homes every year. The goal of the Feline Refuge is to actively demonstrate pet owner responsibility and to circumvent the cycle of animal abuse and domestic violence through juvenile and adult self-esteem programs. It is also their goal to educate and empower caring members of the community and other animal advocacy organizations with practical overpopulation solutions. Their web site has an extensive list of animal related hotlines, providing free or low-cost help.

American Pet Association
PO Box 7172
Boulder, CO 80306-7172
(800) 272-7387
www.apapets.com
e-mail: apa@apapets.org
Lost Pet Hotline: 888-272-3686

The APA is an independent, national humane organization dedicated to promoting responsible pet ownership through action services and education. Founded in 1991, all of the APA's programs are designed to help pet owners and their pets live a more peaceful, safe and enjoyable coexistence. They strive to develop a greater appreciation for the role that pets play in our daily lives. The web site contains very helpful information for pet owners, member services information, humane societies listings, veterinarian finder and Ask the Vet Forum.

American Kennel Club
5580 Centerview Drive
Raleigh, NC 27606
www.akc.org/index.html

AKC's mission is to maintain a registry for pure-bred dogs and preserve its integrity; sanction dog events that promote interest in, and sustain the process of, breeding for type and function of pure-bred dogs; protect and assure the continuation of the sport of purebred dogs. Records the parentage of over one million dogs annually. Sponsors more than 15,000 dog competitions each year held by licensed and member clubs.

Fun Facts About Pets

- Currently, over 55 percent of all American households (52.5 million) have some kind of pet. Thirty-one percent of those have cats, while thirty-seven percent have dogs.

- Cats outnumber dogs in America 55 million to 52 million. While cat ownership has been increasing dramatically over the last decade, dog ownership has been declining. This is because many cat owners have more than one cat and because more people are living in apartments or condominiums which may allow cats but exclude dogs.

- There are approximately 110 million cats and dogs, not to mention all the hamsters, birds, fish, ferrets and other pets.

- One out of every ten U.S. households has a bird; the total number of pet birds is estimated at over 31 million.

- Parakeets are the most popular birds, followed by finches, cockateils, canaries, parrots, love-birds, cockatoos, mynahs, and macaws.

- The average bird owner has three birds and has owned birds for over eight years.

- Seventy-one percent of dog owners buy gifts for their pets.

- House cats live 15 years or longer (45+ years in human years). Occasionally, a cat has been recorded as having lived more then thirty years. Lifespans are expected to lengthen as new breakthroughs are made in nutritional and medical research.

- Three out of seven cats in the U.S. are homeless.

- Fourteen percent of U.S. households now own both cats and dogs together.

- Twenty-three percent of single people own one or more cats, seventeen percent own dogs.

- Forty-six percent of families without children have a cat or dog (thirty-three percent have dogs; twenty-four percent own cats).

- Among families with children ages 6-12, pet ownership jumps to sixty-eight percent (fifty-six percent have at least one dog and thirty-six percent have one or more cats).

- A cat has 130,000 hairs per square inch on its belly.

- Persian cats come in more than fifty different colors.

- Most dogs sleep eleven hours a day.

- Of the seventy-three percent of owners who let their dog sleep in the bedroom, thirty-three percent allow them in bed.

- Sixty-seven percent of dog owners have a picture of them in their wallets.

- Forty percent of dog owners celebrate their pet's birthday every year.

- Sixty-nine percent of dog owners talk to them as if they were people.

- Cocker spaniels are ranked the highest in breed popularity. Followed by Laborador Retrievers, Poodles, Golden Retrievers, Rottweilers, German Shephards, Chow Chows, Dashshunds, Beagles and Miniature Schnauzers.

- Persian cats are the most popular purebreed cat breed. Other are Siamese, Maine coon cats, abyssians, exotic shorthairs, Oriental shorthairs, Scottish folds, Burmese, American shorthairs and Birmans.

More Free Gifts and Incredible Bargains!

Have you reached the golden age of 50? Then you're going to love **Free Stuff & Good Deals for Folks over 50**. It features goods and services that are either absolutely free or are such a fantastic deal, you won't want to pass them up! And best of all, author and professional bargain hunter Linda Bowman shows you how to obtain your free gifts and incredible bargains quickly and easily. This fact-filled guide is packed with information on where to find:

- Free Entertainment
- Incredible Travel Bargains
- Free Health Care Information
- Prescription Medicine Discounts
- Free Financial, Investment and Tax Advice
- Free Educational Opportunities
- Sports, Fitness and Exercise Bargains
- Free Magazines, Newsletters, Catalogs and Books
- Free Medicare and Insurance Information
- Incredible Shopping Bargains
- Organizations and Associations for Folks over 50
. . . and much more!

$12.95
1-800-784-9553

More Free Gifts and Incredible Bargains!

Have you discovered the joy of surfing the World Wide Web? Then you're going to love **Free Stuff & Good Deals on the Internet**. It features goods and services that are either absolutely free or are such a fantastic deal, you won't want to pass them up! And best of all, author and professional bargain hunter Linda Bowman shows you how to obtain your free gifts and incredible bargains quickly and easily. This fact-filled guide is packed with information on where to find:

- Free Money on the Internet
- Free Expert Advice
- Incredible Travel Bargains
- Free Health Care Information
- Free Financial and Legal Advice
- Free Educational Opportunities
- Free Business Opportunities
- Incredible Shopping Bargains
- Free Magazines, Newsletters, Catalogs and Books
- Free Stuff for Kids and Their Parents
- Organizations and Associations
. . . and much more!

$12.95
1-800-784-9553

BOOK DESCRIPTIONS

The Book of Good Habits
Simple and Creative Ways to Enrich Your Life
by Dirk Mathison
224 pages $9.95

Café Nation
Coffee Folklore, Magick, and Divination
by Sandra Mizumoto Posey
224 pages $9.95

Collecting Sins
A Novel
by Steven Sobel
288 pages $13

FREE Stuff & Good Deals for Folks over 50
by Linda Bowman
240 pages $12.95

FREE Stuff & Good Deals for Your Pet
by Linda Bowman
240 pages $12.95

FREE Stuff & Good Deals on the Internet
by Linda Bowman
240 pages $12.95

Health Care Handbook
A Consumer's Guide to the American Health Care System
by Mark Cromer
256 pages $12.95

Helpful Household Hints
The Ultimate Guide to Housekeeping
by June King
224 pages $12.95

How To Find Your Family Roots and Write Your Family History
by William Latham and Cindy Higgins
288 pages $14.95

How To Win Lotteries, Sweepstakes, and Contests in the 21st Century
by Steve "America's Sweepstakes King" Ledoux
224 pages $14.95

Letter Writing Made Easy!
Featuring Sample Letters for Hundreds of Common Occasions
by Margaret McCarthy
224 pages $12.95

Letter Writing Made Easy! Volume 2
Featuring More Sample Letters for Hundreds of Common Occasions
by Margaret McCarthy
224 pages $12.95

Nancy Shavick's Tarot Universe
by Nancy Shavick
336 pages $15.95

Offbeat Food
Adventures in an Omnivorous World
by Alan Ridenour
240 pages $19.95

Offbeat Golf
A Swingin' Guide To a Worldwide Obsession
by Bob Loeffelbein
192 pages $17.95

Offbeat Marijuana
The Life and Times of the World's Grooviest Plant
by Saul Rubin
240 pages $19.95

Offbeat Museums
The Collections and Curators of America's Most Unusual Museums
by Saul Rubin
240 pages $19.95

Past Imperfect
How Tracing Your Family Medical History Can Save Your Life
by Carol Daus
240 pages $12.95

Quack!
Tales of Medical Fraud from the Museum of Questionable Medical Devices
by Bob McCoy
240 pages $19.95

The Seven Sacred Rites of Menopause
The Spiritual Journey to the Wise-Woman Years
by Kristi Meisenbach Boylan
144 pages $11.95

Silent Echoes
Discovering Early Hollywood Through the Films of Buster Keaton
by John Bengtson
240 pages $24.95

What's Buggin' You?
Michael Bohdan's Guide to Home Pest Control
by Michael Bohdan
256 pages $12.95

ORDER FORM
1-800-784-9553

	Quantity	Amount
The Book of Good Habits ($9.95)	_____	_____
Café Nation ($9.95)	_____	_____
Collecting Sins ($13)	_____	_____
FREE Stuff & Good Deals for Folks over 50 ($12.95)	_____	_____
FREE Stuff & Good Deals for Your Pet ($12.95)	_____	_____
FREE Stuff & Good Deals on the Internet ($12.95)	_____	_____
Health Care Handbook ($12.95)	_____	_____
Helpful Household Hints ($12.95)	_____	_____
How to Find Your Family Roots . . . ($14.95)	_____	_____
How to Win Lotteries, Sweepstakes, and Contests . . . ($14.95)	_____	_____
Letter Writing Made Easy! ($12.95)	_____	_____
Letter Writing Made Easy! Volume 2 ($12.95)	_____	_____
Nancy Shavick's Tarot Universe ($15.95)	_____	_____
Offbeat Food ($19.95)	_____	_____
Offbeat Golf ($17.95)	_____	_____
Offbeat Marijuana ($19.95)	_____	_____
Offbeat Museums ($19.95)	_____	_____
Past Imperfect ($12.95)	_____	_____
Quack! ($19.95)	_____	_____
The Seven Sacred Rites of Menopause ($11.95)	_____	_____
Silent Echoes ($24.95)	_____	_____
What's Buggin' You? ($12.95)	_____	_____

Shipping & Handling:	
1 book	$3.00
Each additional book is	$ .50

Subtotal _____

CA residents add 8% sales tax _____

Shipping and Handling (see left) _____

TOTAL _____

Name _____

Address _____

City _____ State _____ Zip _____

❏ Visa ❏ MasterCard   Card No.: _____

Exp. Date _____   Signature _____

❏ Enclosed is my check or money order payable to:

Santa Monica Press LLC
P.O. Box 1076
Santa Monica, CA 90406
www.santamonicapress.com

1-800-784-9553